Did You Know...

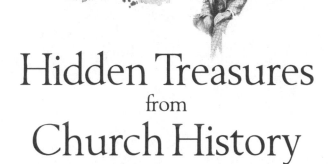

Hidden Treasures
from
Church History

JUDY FRASER

To Keith, Craig, and Lisa.

Published and Distributed by:

Granite Publishing and Distribution, L.L.C.
270 S. Mountainlands Dr.
Orem, UT 84058
(801) 229-9023

Photos:
    Camilla Eyring Kimball courtesy of Edward Kimball.
    Harold B. Lee courtesy of Helen Lee Goates.
    Joseph Fielding Smith and Jessie Evans Smith courtesy of
        Joseph Fielding McConkie.
    Norman Vincent Peale courtesy of Mrs. Ruth Stafford Peale.
    All other photos courtesy of LDS Church Archives.

Special thanks to Bill Slaugher and April Williamsen.
Cover Artist: Lisa Fraser
Cover Design and Typeset by: SunRise Publishing, Orem, Utah

ISBN: 1-57636-023-7

TABLE OF CONTENTS

PREFACE

The history of The Church of Jesus Christ of Latter-day Saints is closely intertwined with the personal histories of its members and leaders. Those who created the foundation we now build upon were as individual and different from each other as we are today. Each had circumstances and personality traits which were like no other. Yet the people written about in this book had one thing in common: A deep and abiding testimony that this is the work of the Lord, and a commitment to put His gospel first in their lives, whatever the cost.

Learning about these men and women has been a fascinating experience for me and has strengthened my faith, and I hope it will do so for the reader.

For the pleasure of the reader, we have avoided footnotes and have, instead, presented a brief bibliography at the end of the book that indicates the sources used in preparing this work.

Chapter One
THE GOOD HUSBAND

Miriam's husband had led a hard frontiersman's life. He grew up constantly grubbing for a living off the land, his family moving often and starting all over again in hopes of better prospects. Miriam's husband had almost no formal education. His spelling was so atrocious that it was an embarrassment to him. His poverty-stricken upbringing had left him no time to read great authors, to learn the social graces, or to do anything but focus on survival. Many times as a boy he had done hard manual labor on an empty stomach.

Years before he was born his mother had contracted tuberculosis. He and his brothers learned to do her "women's work" as a matter of necessity. He had grown up making bread, washing dishes, milking cows and making butter for the family, as well as doing the outside work. His family had never prospered—neighbors said they just seemed to attract bad luck.

But when the young man met his attractive blonde, blue-eyed Miriam, he hoped that with her at his side a happier future would be his. They married, but the happy future was not to be, for she too contracted tuberculosis. Tragic, familiar history repeated itself as Miriam's young husband again took up his well-rehearsed routine. Daily he prepared breakfast, tenderly carried Miriam from the bed to the chair by the table, sat her there and did the dishes after they ate. Then he would dress baby Vilate and help six-year-old Elizabeth to dress. He would carry Miriam to the chair in front of the fire, then do other necessary household chores before leaving for his day's work. Getting these "home" chores done often meant earning a living only part-time.

Even so, Miriam's husband was good at his vocation. He

was a first-rate carpenter, much in demand in the area for building homes, making mantels, making all kinds of furniture and beautiful fanlight doorways, and crafting whatever neighbors needed. He also did glazing (cutting glass for windows) and painting.

His heavy load and the many hardships of his life sometimes caused Miriam's husband to feel discouraged. He wondered where the purpose was in his life. Then one day he heard the doctrines of Joseph Smith preached. Initially he was cynical, as he was toward all professed religionists. However in time he began to believe the message. He had found the truth, and he and Miriam were baptized. They now found hope and meaning in their lives, despite their trials. His despondency left and never returned.

Miriam's condition continued to worsen, but she was thankful to have found the gospel in this life. When she died, the children were left in the care of friends as the young widower traveled throughout the area, teaching the restored gospel. A year and a half after Miriam's death, he remarried.

Miriam didn't live to see her husband develop his talents fully. He glazed the windows for the Kirtland Temple and oversaw the finishing details. In Salt Lake he fashioned the exquisite chandelier in the Salt Lake Theatre. But it would not be for these talents that he would be known; it would be for his extraordinary leadership skills. Like Moses, he would lead a people to their promised land. Then he would colonize that promised land and continue to lead them for over thirty years. Miriam Works was the first of many wives; her kind husband was Brigham Young.

Brigham Young became the second president of the church on Dec. 27, 1847. He served for nearly thirty years, until his death on August 29, 1877. He served several missions, presided as the pioneers came to Utah, and sent people to colonize a large area of the west. His administration was the longest in church history.

Photo: *Brigham Young*

Chapter Two
THE REFUGEE

The young woman lived a happy life. She was a high school student in the Mormon colony of Juarez in Mexico. The work ethic of the Mormon settlers had turned the colony into a prosperous place, of which she was very proud. It had a co-op store, a tannery and gristmill, with a lumber company nearby. Her father was one of the colony's most prominent and prosperous citizens, owning a ranch with many horses and cattle. Their family had a phone with which they ordered items from the co-op and had them delivered. The seventeen-year-old girl worked with her family to provide their home with stored food. They bottled fruits and vegetables; they salted pork and beans in barrels. They stored fresh fruits and vegetables in the cellar, and flour and grain in the granary.

The summer of 1912 was a blackberry summer for the young woman's family. The berries grew abundantly and one sweltering July Saturday they sweated through bottling 100 quarts. The girl's hard work would be worthwhile, for she anticipated the coming year, when the blackberries would provide a special treat with their meals.

Revolution had been fomenting in the Mexican colonies for some time that summer, yet so far it seemed that the Saints were secure and would not be bothered. Suddenly things took a bad turn, and the young woman found out about it that Saturday night after bottling the berries.

Her father came home to tell the family that they must leave Juarez for the United States the next day without him. He assured them this would be a temporary move. Stake leaders felt it best to send the women and children to El Paso, Texas until things cooled down, which they hoped wouldn't be long.

The young woman's father pried up the floorboards on the porch. She and her mother quickly transferred the 100 glistening bottles of dark berries into the space underneath the porch. They replaced the floorboards and nailed them down securely. Then the girl helped hide their valuables wherever she could, hoping that despite the revolution she would soon return and find everything intact.

The young woman would be leaving the next day with her family of thirteen: Her pregnant mother, her brothers and sisters, her father's other wife and their children, and her grandmother. They could pack only one trunk for them all. The teenage girl had saved her dolls, her school papers and all her childhood toys, but she could take none of these with her.

Sunday morning came, and the family drove their buggy eight miles to the train station. The area was packed with hundreds of people and their wagons and buggies. Mexican revolutionaries rode arrogantly through the crowd, stealing what they wanted, with no opposition from the frightened people.

The young woman boarded the train with her family, waving goodbye to her father. As the train moved along, more people boarded, until the cars became packed in the intense and unrelenting heat.

The 150-mile trip to El Paso was a tense one for all. The train traveled slowly and often stopped. Surely the rebels would intercept it at some point. It crawled along all through that day and into the night, until at dawn the teenager finally saw the U.S. flag. She was so relieved to be safe at last. Everyone in the crowded cars cheered.

After she reached El Paso the young woman and her family were taken to a lumberyard which had been turned into a temporary shelter. Leaving her home was bad enough. The suffering of the train ride was bad enough. But the proud girl couldn't believe what was next. She knew she should be grateful for shelter, but she was appalled at the conditions in which they were expected to stay.

The girl's family was directed to a large corral filled with refugees. The corral was hot, dusty, fly-ridden and noisy. One stall was their whole family's accommodation. They put up blankets for privacy. Five women gave birth in the corral that night.

The next day the girl felt like she was on display in a zoo. The people of El Paso stared and pointed at them. Newsmen and photographers, in search of a good story, roamed everywhere. The girl felt humiliated and wanted only to get out of there. She was relieved when her mother found a little hotel room for them all. Their ordeal wasn't over, for the room had no windows and was almost unbearable in the July heat. At least it was private. Grandma slept on the bed and everyone else on the floor, some under the bed.

Knowing this was a temporary situation helped the girl to bear the discomfort. She reasoned that Father would come and get them any day now and take them home. Life would go on as usual and this would be just a distant memory.

Yet in a week, her father still hadn't come, and they, along with other refugees, moved to a larger tenement with more room and a place for the children to play outside. Government representatives brought food to the Mormon refugees daily.

It was an uncertain time and the seventeen-year-old tried to keep her mind and hands busy. She was the oldest child in her family and helped care for her younger brothers and sisters. She also spent many hours sitting on her bedroll doing embroidery.

Still the days passed slowly and it began to look as if her father would not be there right away. The restless teenager pleaded with her mother to let her get a job, as several others her age were doing. Finally her mother relented and she got a job as a maid for a wealthy family, happy to be doing something and earning money for it.

Then her father came. Conditions had worsened in Mexico. Their stake president had decided that the men couldn't defend their homes and other property without some loss of life. Still they hoped everyone could return. Her father rented a house and the girl worked for a sick lady near them.

Weeks passed as the anxious family waited for word that they could return home. They hoped the revolution would soon bypass their area and that when they got back, not much would have been taken from them. Finally they realized that it would be a long time before they could go home and perhaps never.

The teenager saw her father go back home several times trying to transport some of his cattle to the U.S. He was never able to do so. Virtually everything they owned was in Mexico, so the family was now destitute. As she ate the plain food the young woman probably imagined how delicious those black-berries would have tasted and wondered if some revolutionary had ever found the cache, and was enjoying them now.

Though she was still young, her parents could no longer support the young woman. They decided that since the government offered free train tickets out of Texas to the refugees, the girl would go to Utah to finish high school. Kind relatives there could take her in and she would work for her board. Education was very important to her family, and the girl hoped to go on to college and eventually get a good-paying teaching job.

The seventeen-year-old had many adjustments and adventures ahead of her in Utah. She worked hard and adapted to her situation. Camilla Eyring Kimball supported herself until she married several years later.

Camilla Eyring's family never returned to Mexico. Camilla went to Utah, where she lived with relatives and friends and graduated from high school. At age nineteen she became a high school home economics teacher. She later taught at Gila Academy in Thatcher, Arizona. When she was nearly twenty-three years old she married Spencer W. Kimball and they had four children. He later became the twelfth president of the Church.

Photo: *Camilla Eyring*

Chapter Three

THE PROPHET AND HIS FRIEND

The prophet Joseph's friend William was a talented, multi-faceted man. He was a well-educated newspaper editor and active in politics. One day he bought a Book of Mormon from Parley P. Pratt. He read it with his wife that night, comparing its teachings with the Bible. The next morning William told his wife: "I am going to join that church; I am convinced that it is true." He felt that the Book of Mormon was a "glorious treasure."

A year later William met Joseph Smith in Kirtland and told him he wanted to "do the will of the Lord." He told the prophet that "notwithstanding my body was not baptized into this church, yet my heart was here from the time I became acquainted with the Book of Mormon."

William was baptized and confirmed, and began at once to use his many talents in the service of the gospel. The prophet directed him to take his family to Independence, Missouri. There William set up the church printing press and published the first church newspaper in Independence. He was a powerful, convincing writer. He helped choose and publish the revelations in the Book of Commandments, and also wrote several hymns. William also served as an agent and clerk for the Prophet in Independence.

Unfortunately, the Jackson county mobs also recognized the power of his press. They destroyed the press as well as his family's home, and threatened to kill all the Saints. William joined with five other men to offer his life as ransom for the Saints, to be scourged or killed. The mob rejected their offer.

The Saints were forced to move to the area of Far West, and William was called to be in the Stake Presidency there.

Sadly, he and the other two members of the presidency were charged with misusing church funds, and were excommunicated.

William turned very bitter. He now saw the prophet Joseph as his enemy and vowed to destroy him. William joined others in persecuting the church, signing an affidavit against the prophet and other church leaders. His actions helped fuel the fire of anti-Mormon feeling which culminated in the prophet's five-month imprisonment and the severe suffering of all the Saints.

But, unlike most other apostates, William humbled himself. In great sorrow for what he had done, two years later he wrote to Joseph in Nauvoo:

> Brother Joseph, ... I am as the prodigal son.
>
> I know my situation, you know it, and God knows it, and I want to be saved if my friends will help me.... I have done wrong and I am sorry. The beam is in my own eye. I have not walked along with my friends according to my holy anointing. I ask forgiveness in the name of Jesus Christ of all the Saints, for I will do right, God helping me. I want your fellowship; if you cannot grant that, grant me your peace and friendship, for we are brethren, and our communion used to be sweet, and whenever the Lord brings us together again, I will make all the satisfaction on every point that Saints or God can require.

The prophet wrote back:

> ...We have suffered much in consequence of your behavior—the cup of gall, already full enough for mortals to drink, was indeed filled to overflowing when you turned against us.
>
> However, the cup has been drunk, the will of our Father has been done, and we are yet alive, for which we thank the Lord and having been delivered from the hands of wicked men by the mercy of our God, we say it is your privilege to be delivered from the powers of the adversary, be brought into the liberty of God's dear children, and again take your stand among the Saints of the Most High, and by diligence, humility, and love

unfeigned, commend yourself to our God, and your God, and to the Church of Jesus Christ.

Believing your confession to be real, and your repentance genuine, I shall be happy once again to give you the right hand of fellowship, and rejoice over the returning prodigal.

'Come on, dear brother, since the war is past, for friends at first, are friends again at last.'

Less than four years later William preached the Prophet's funeral sermon. Throughout his life he wrote words to several hymns we still sing today, but none is more stirring than his tribute to his friend, the Prophet Joseph:

> Great is his glory and endless his Priesthood.
> Ever and ever the keys he will hold.
> Faithful and true, he will enter his kingdom,
> Crowned in the midst of the prophets of old.

In writing "Praise to the Man," William Wines Phelps created a lasting memorial proving forever that he was, indeed, loyal to his friend.

W.W. Phelps was a prolific writer. He wrote the words to several hymns, including: "The Spirit of God," "Now Let Us Rejoice," "Redeemer of Israel," "Gently Raise the Sacred Strain," and "O God, the Eternal Father."

Photo: *W. W. Phelps*

Chapter Four
THE HERD BOY

The nine-year-old boy disliked Winter Quarters intense-
ly. Nauvoo was the only other home he could remember, and this was nothing like beautiful Nauvoo. Here hundreds
had died from scurvy and other diseases, so he was accurate in
calling it a "sickly hole." He lived for the day when he could
leave Winter Quarters for the valleys of the mountains.
Anything that might delay his family's departure was more to
be feared than death itself, which is why he faced the Indians
with such uncommon boldness one day.

In Winter Quarters everyone worked hard. This boy's job
was to herd the cattle, which included the cows, young calves,
and several yoke of oxen not being used. On this particular day
he went out with three other boys to their accustomed herding
place, about two miles from Winter Quarters.

Two of the boys in their group were near his own age
(nine) and the fourth was a serious-minded teenager. The
teenager, who seemed so ancient to the others, decided that
he'd take a different route to the herding grounds that day in
order to gather some nuts on the way. This pleased the younger
boys, because they felt he put a damper on their fun.

The three young boys rode their horses in high spirits that
day. They were, in fact, feeling so good that the herd boy and
his friend teased the third until he went home angrily. The two
who were left got to their destination, a spring, and set down
their dinner pails. Their cattle grazed contentedly while the
two boys exuberantly raced their horses and jumped them
across ditches, waiting for the teenager to join them.

Suddenly about a half mile ahead, across a grassy rolling
area, appeared a group of Indians on horseback. They wore

15

only breechcloths; their bodies and faces were covered with frightening war paint. They whooped as they raced toward the cattle and the two boys.

The herd boy was startled to see his companion turn and run for home, yelling, "Indians, Indians!!". Now the herd boy was alone.

In a few short seconds he must decide what to do. He thought of his dream of going west, and of how these cattle would be crucial for that journey. If these Indians succeeded in driving them off, he would have to stay in Winter Quarters! The possibility of death paled in comparison.

He spurred his horse and rode full speed toward the cattle, which were halfway between him and the Indians. He raced to them, hoping they would stampede toward home before the Indians reached them. Arriving just as the Indians did, he turned his horse around to return home, while yelling at the cattle to follow him. Between his loud yells and the Indians' whoops, the frightened animals began to stampede toward home.

The boy was now riding back the way he had come, with the Indians in full pursuit on all sides, trying to head him off, with the cattle ahead of them all. Some of the Indians had split off earlier and were now ahead of him, coming in on either side repeatedly, forcing him to change direction. His horse became winded. He could dodge them no longer.

Finally the herd boy was overtaken by the skillful horse-men. One rode on his right and one on his left, each grabbing an arm and a leg of the hapless boy, and jerking him off his horse. They slowed down until his horse ran out from under him; then they threw him ferociously to the ground. As the boy lay there several horses ran over him, but miraculously he was unhurt. At this point a few white men appeared in the distance, holding pitchforks. (They had been on their way to the hay-fields and heard the other boy's screaming.) At their appear-ance the Indians rode off as quickly as they'd come.

The herd boy gingerly stood up. Once he could walk again

he went after the other boy, whom the Indians had chased in the fracas. When he reached the hill he saw his friend walking toward town and was thankful for his safety. When the boy reached town, a lot of people were gathering in the bowery, the first boy having told them what had happened. In the crowd were the nine-year-old's mother and brothers and sisters, very relieved to see him alive and well.

The men formed two "posses," one on horseback to chase the Indians, and one on foot, to track down the cattle, with the two boys leading them. Unbeknownst to the latter group, the teenage boy had finally come to the spring after the excitement was over, found the cattle, and herded them home by a different road.

Because of this, the group couldn't find the cattle anywhere. After hours of searching in vain, the herd boy finally trudged back to Winter Quarters, certain that after all his exertion and danger, he would still be stuck for the rest of his life in Winter Quarters. He was overjoyed to reach town and find that the cattle were all there and taken care of.

In the spring of 1848 the herd boy's family left Winter Quarters, and as he drove one of the teams that carried their belongings he probably didn't even look back. The precious cattle and oxen he had saved were his ticket to a new and better home. Indeed, many adventures lay ahead for the boy. He was Joseph F. (Fielding) Smith, son of the martyred Hyrum Smith and Mary Fielding Smith.

Joseph F. Smith was the sixth president of the Church. He served seventeen years, from October 17, 1901, to November 19, 1918. During his presidency he suffered through a strong anti-Mormon vendetta in the media. This was directed not only at the Church, but at him personally. He forgave those who ridiculed and caricatured him.

Photo: *Joseph F. Smith*

Chapter Five

JEDDY

His widowed mother's only son, Jeddy knew what it was to live in poverty. When he was seven years old his late father's estate was settled and he and his mother moved out of their spacious home into a small adobe house. She sewed and took in boarders to make ends meet. The roof often leaked and Jeddy helped put buckets in strategic places. He remembered times when they only had four pounds of sugar to last an entire year, and when butter was a luxury he rarely tasted. One Christmas his mother cried because she couldn't even afford to buy him a stick of candy.

It has been said that initiative is the instinctive response to lack, and perhaps because of the poverty of his youth, there grew within Jeddy a strong drive to make money and to give his mother a more comfortable life. She told him she would support him when he was young and he could support her when she was old.

Even in his boyhood Jeddy began to show business "smarts". He blacked boots for his mother's boarders at a nickel a pair. He became an expert marble player and won so many marbles that he could hire other boys to do his household chores. He wanted to see the plays at the Salt Lake Theatre but was unable to afford a ticket, so he worked there carrying water to patrons in the balcony.

Jeddy began doing accounting in an insurance office at age fifteen. After hours he made greeting cards as a sideline, sometimes making more money on the cards than on his regular job. He also did bookkeeping for a bank and several other companies. By age twenty he was selling insurance and had his fingers in several business 'pies'. Because of his confidence and business savvy, the men with whom he worked seemed unaware of his youth.

Jeddy started a life insurance company, at a time when life insurance was fairly new. He believed wholeheartedly in the product he sold, knowing firsthand what it was to grow up in an impoverished widow's home. Jeddy strongly wanted to save others from the hardship that could come when the breadwinner died. During his life he also participated in many other business ventures which would benefit church members. He felt that "home industries" kept money where it would benefit local members rather than others. This, he believed, was an important part of building up Zion. Some of the businesses he invested in and promoted were: banking, mining, ranching, soap-making, the manufacture of vinegar, beekeeping, and the sugar industry.

Jeddy thoroughly enjoyed making money, and just as thoroughly, using it to help those in need. He began supporting his mother while he was still in his youth. Being particularly aware of the plight of the widow, he paid off the mortgages of many a widow. He helped find jobs and get medical attention for their family members when needed. However, he didn't stop with widows. Jeddy helped missionaries. He hired genealogists who needed work to research his line, and then he did temple work for his deceased ancestors. He helped his extended family get into homes. He gave money to people he'd heard were in need, even though he'd never met them.

Jeddy had many strong character traits and was doggedly determined to succeed in his business dealings, so it's interesting that in his youth he was sometimes underestimated by his church leaders.

When Jeddy's bishop offered to buy his mother a new roof out of fast offering funds she declined. She proudly told the bishop that her son would build her a new home when he grew up. The bishop guffawed at that, saying that if she were to wait for Jeddy to do so, she would wait forever. After all, her son was the laziest boy in the ward! When at age twenty-one Jeddy had that home built for her, he invited the bishop to offer the dedicatory prayer. He also thanked the bishop for his earlier comments. These, he said, had stimulated him to build the home more quickly than he might have done without that goad. The bishop apologized and declared Jeddy the hardest worker in the ward. He had come to love his young friend.

Again Jeddy was misjudged when, one month short of his twenty-fourth birthday, he was called to be a stake president. John Taylor was president of the church. He and his counselor Joseph F. Smith were the presiding authorities at the meeting where Jeddy was called. Jeddy's short (seven-and-a-half minute) talk at that meeting prompted a comment later on, after the meeting, as the three ate. President Smith asked why Jeddy had not borne his testimony during his talk. Jeddy promptly answered that it was because he believed the church was true but didn't feel he knew. President Smith turned to President Taylor. He suggested that maybe at the afternoon session of stake conference they had better undo what they had just done in the morning session! Jeddy replied that that would be fine with him—he had never sought this office. President Taylor laughed and defused the situation, "He has a testimony all right, he just doesn't know it yet." (It wasn't long before Jeddy was bearing testimony.) As the years passed, Jeddy and President Smith became very close friends, and President Smith grew to love and appreciate him.

With all the church responsibilities that came his way, Jeddy continued to be involved in business activities. He was financially secure until the Panic of 1891-1893 in which several businesses in which he was involved left him with a heavy load of debt. Even though friends counseled him to take out bankruptcy, he refused, thereby suffering for many years under that worrisome burden. It was lifted only when he accepted a call to serve as mission president in Japan. During the months before he left, he was miraculously able to make enough to pay off all his debts. He later strongly cautioned church members to stay out of debt, speaking from personal experience as well as inspiration. Many who chose not to follow this counsel grew to bitterly regret it when the Great Depression of the 1930s came.

Jeddy's lifetime spanned many changes in the world. As a child he had played with Brigham Young's grandchildren in the Lion House and knew President Young well. He died in the waning months of World War II. He was the youngest stake president in the church when he was sustained a month short of his twenty-fourth birthday. He was ordained an apostle when not yet twenty-six years old, and became church president at age sixty-two. Heber Jeddy Grant was the prophet who led the church through the Great Depression and World War II, and passed away as the war was drawing to a close.

Heber J. Grant was the seventh president of the church. He served for twenty-six years, from November 23, 1918, until his death on May 14, 1945, which made his administration the second longest. During his presidency he won the friendship and admiration of many outside the church, which helped dispel prejudice against church members.

Top Photo: *Heber J. Grant with his mother, Rachel Ivins Grant*
Bottom Photo: *Heber J. Grant*

Chapter Six

THE GREAT ESCAPE

The jail in Columbia, Missouri, was certainly nothing like home. Even so, it was more comfortable than the Richmond jail, with which Parker was well acquainted. He had been arrested in November in Far West and taken to Richmond, where he spent all winter in that cold, dark and filthy dungeon. He was guarded by men who brandished loaded pistols. The guards were vulgar, crude drunks who delighted in boasting of their obscene and criminal acts, which made the jail feel even more like a hell. The guards told Parker daily that he would be assassinated and would never leave the state alive. His family had visited him there and even stayed with him at times during the winter to try to make his life a little more bearable. Then spring came and they had to leave for Far West in order to get help in moving to Illinois.

Parker's despair with his situation grew until he began fasting and praying fervently to know only one thing: not when he would be released, or how it might happen, just if he would ever again be free. Then one night his deceased first wife came to him in a vision, to tell him that, yes, he would be free again. Then Parker wanted to know more—how would it happen? She hadn't been given that information, and he was sorry for asking. But her presence and her message comforted him.

With spring came hope. Parker had a change of venue, was moved to this new jail, in Columbia, and hoped that he would finally be able to get due process of law and be released to go home. His accommodations were better here. He was forced to sleep in the "dungeon" only at night. During the day he was imprisoned in the more comfortable upper room. In contrast to Richmond, there was only one jailer here, who lived in two other rooms of the prison with his family. What a relief it was to be free of the cruel boasts of the drunken guards.

Some of his fellow prisoners had been set free, now leaving only Morris Phelps, King Follett, and Parker, not including "Luman" and "Phila." Luman, a vulgar, hard-faced man, had apostatized while in jail and now was a great friend of their enemies. He spied on his fellow prisoners in exchange for more freedom. He went out to eat with the law enforcement officers, or to spend a day with his wife whenever he desired.

Luman's wife, Phila, sometimes came to spend a few days with him in the jail. She was a coarse, ugly woman. Yet, inexplicably, Luman feared that other men found Phila lovely and desirable, and he was insanely jealous of her. His jealousy made him abusive of her. Whenever she was there, there would be constant fighting. That made life more miserable for the prisoners, but also provided comic relief: When the lovebirds made up, their angry fighting words turned to syrupy sweet ones!

Parker begrudged Luman and Phila their special treatment. Not only did they get time outside the jail, but were allowed to stay at night in the more comfortable upper room while the other three had to sleep on the floor of the "dungeon." But at least now when the two fought all night the others could get some rest. That had not been the case in Richmond, when they were all in the same cell day and night and sometimes didn't sleep all night because of the fighting.

Parker was the only Church leader still in Missouri. Friends told him that the others who had been captured with him had already escaped and were safely in Illinois. Joseph and Hyrum and their companions arrived in Illinois in April. Governor Boggs threatened with death any Mormons who didn't leave Missouri, and as an apostle, Parker was in particular danger.

Yet Joseph told them, before they were separated, that it had been revealed to him that no matter how they suffered, none of them would lose their lives. Parker hung on to that promise through all the cold, dark months. Now, as spring turned into summer, he was blessed with a vision of how he would make his escape. It was given to him twice.

Morris' wife came to visit and she, too, received this revelation. She and the three prisoners sat around and talked with joy of that day when they would make their escape, being careful to discuss it only when Luman and Phila were gone. Parker, who was so ill he could hardly stand, was administered to and healed, enabling him to take part in the escape planning.

The plan took form. In their escape they would have three accomplices: Parker's brother, Morris' wife, and her brother. The three horses brought by the visitors would become the "getaway vehicles." The three accomplices visited the prisoners for several days and each person planned and practiced his part to perfection. Parker knew that if the others were caught their lives would probably be spared, but if he were caught he would probably be killed, because of his position in the church. Even so, after what seemed like a lifetime in prison (over eight months) he would make the attempt or die trying!

D-day: July 4th, 1839. The plotters had torn up an old shirt and made a "flag" of sorts with it. On the white background they sewed a red eagle and the word "LIBERTY" in red block letters. They exulted in their hopes for this memorable day. They tied their pennant to a pole and proudly hung it out their upper window.

People from all around came to Columbia, Missouri, on the 4th for the holiday festivities. The jail was next to the public square, and during the day hundreds of people walked by the flag, read its message, and laughed. "Liberty!" The foolishness of those Mormons! How ironic it was for men who had been imprisoned for so many months to fly a flag with that word, of all words! Some boys admired the crude banner and asked if they could have it, and the prisoners told them they could have it the next day. The flag had become their rallying-cry. When people mocked their flag the prisoners laughed, too. They hoped the joke would be on the citizens.

All day cannons blasted, bands played, people celebrated, but none more than Parker and his comrades. They'd received permission to make and eat a special meal, and with their visiting friends they celebrated with gusto. After this repast their friends bade them hearty, loud goodbyes, with promises to give messages to loved ones and to continue the legal processes in motion for their releases. This, they hoped, would fool the 'spies' and the jailer into a false sense of security. The two male visitors then left, taking the three horses into the woods about a half mile away. They waited there. Morris' wife stayed behind, where she would be safe, to aid in the escape with her prayers.

Late afternoon came. Tensions increased in the prison cell. Parker knew they would have to execute their plan before nightfall because, when dusk came, they would be put down in the "dungeon" to sleep. Their plan hinged on one weakness in the upper cell: There was a heavy, bolted door outside the cell, and then an inner door after that. The inner door had a hole in it for passing food through. However the coffeepot the jailer brought up nightly for their supper was too big to be put through the hole easily. The jailer burned his fingers if he tried to do so, so he often just opened the inner door to pass it through. Their escape depended on the jailer's opening that inner door.

The sun sank lower in the sky; celebrations outside were winding down. Occasionally the sounds of a drum or a bugle wafted through the warm night air. Parker felt the adrenalin surge through his body. He knew that the rest of his life depended upon the events of the next few minutes. After months of imprisonment, he would try or die in the attempt.

At last he heard the sounds of the jailer clumping up the wooden stairs. Morris, an ex-wrestler, positioned himself behind the door to come out first. Parker was poised to run right behind him. Brother Follett would open the door, they would burst out and he would follow.

The jailer opened the outer door. Then he passed the meal

through the hole in the inner door and started passing the coffeepot through. The others held their breaths as Parker asked, "Why don't you open the door, so you don't burn your fingers?" The jailer acquiesced. He turned the key in the lock and Brother Follett flung open the door against the wall. The three men ran down the stairs, Mrs. Phelps praying all the time. The jailer tried to stop them with his arms, but was knocked over and trampled as they ran. The jailer's wife loudly cried out, alerting the people out in the square. As Parker reached the exterior, people were already gathering and gawking.

Fenced fields spread between the jail and the woods a half mile away where the horses waited. Parker ran desperately toward these fields on weak legs which had hardly walked for months. Everywhere crowds gathered. Men, women, and children yelled and swore. Men picked up clubs, sticks, guns or whatever they could find and ran after him and his two friends. Soldiers and riflemen were in hot pursuit. Boys and their dogs chased the escapee, jumping and breaking down fences to do so. Everywhere on the surrounding roads men ran. Parker and his two buddies barely stayed ahead.

After a solid half-mile sprint he saw his brother and Mrs. Phelps' brother in the trees and they urgently pressed him to hurry, as he mounted and reined in his horse:

"Fly quickly, they're upon you!"
"Which way shall we go?"
"Anywhere you can; you're already nearly surrounded!"
"But what will you do? They'll kill you if they can't catch us."
"We'll take care of ourselves; hurry! Now!!"

It was every man for himself. Parker dug his spurs into the horse's flanks and galloped away, leaving the town behind. Immediately he was charged by a man with a gun, with others following behind him. Parker turned the other way, into a thicket, and rode for his life. Gaining distance, he could only hear their dogs barking faintly.

As he rode further Parker realized that he was coming to a road and could hear horse's hooves and men's voices. Turning back into the woods, he felt safe. He dismounted and tied his horse. He climbed a tree and sat in its fork, supporting his arms in another fork, hoping to hide until the commotion had died down and darkness came. There, because of all his exertions, he lay for some time, weak and helpless. He could hardly breathe for awhile, then vomited. After eight months' imprisonment and the resultant weakness, only a miracle had brought him this far. Now he was beyond exhaustion. After resting awhile, he began to pray that he might be able to continue to elude his captors and find safety.

Although Parker could still hear the sounds of horses, men, and dogs looking for him, he was happy that it was getting darker and darker because it increased his chances for safety. A cloudy, moonless night was on his side, as well as the thick foliage of the forest around him. He finally came down from the tree, only to find that his horse had broken free and was gone. Taking a drink from a muddy stream, he began the long walk home.

Trudging in the dark along the highway, he realized that he didn't know this part of Missouri at all and would have only the North Star for navigation. His destination in Illinois was northward over 100 miles. His life was in danger every moment in Missouri. Filled with anxiety and apprehension, he worried about his fellow prisoners and their accomplices. He worried about his physical condition. How would he stand up physically under the rigors of his journey? How could he travel without stopping anywhere to ask for help? How could he cross the Mississippi when all the ferries would be watched? At the same time, he anticipated the joy, if he survived, of seeing his beloved family and friends once again.

Parker walked most of the night, stopping only briefly to sleep. The new day was cloudy, covering his guiding star. He had no idea where he was or what direction he was traveling.

Wary and cautious, he still couldn't help noticing the beauties of the summer day, after his long confinement. In contrast to the fetid prison odors were the sweet smells of wildflowers blooming everywhere. No more would he hear the caterwauling of Luman and Phila. Now he listened in rapture to the profuse birdsongs all around him. He saw deer and wild turkey and heard wolves howling in the distance. He took a deep breath of the bracing, fresh air. He was free!

Parker's first breakfast in freedom was a small biscuit he had stuffed in his pocket. He washed it down with stream water. This was the happiest moment of his life. What if he didn't know where he was; at least nobody else did, either!

Continuing on, Parker asked a woman the way to Columbia (from where he'd just come) then went in the opposite direction. He did his best but was soon lost once more in the forest. It started raining. Soon he was soaked and hungry. He trampled through the forests and grasses in the rain until it was once more dusk. Somehow he must find an overnight shelter if he would be strong enough to make it home. To be seen without a horse would create suspicion, so as he approached a man in front of a house the fugitive said that his horse had run away with all his gear. The man and his wife were glad to put him up, and Parker ate well and slept well.

The second day of his escape dawned sunny. As he ate breakfast with his host family, he played his part well: He was an Indiana farmer who was furious about the loss of his horse. After sharing their meal with him, they gave him food to carry with him, and he was on his way once more.

Walking along the road, Parker found fresh horse tracks and surmised that one of his pursuers had been that way. (He later learned he was right.) He spent all day and the next in a more densely populated part of the state, with which he was somewhat familiar, traveling mostly at night and only very carefully during the day.

By the third or fourth day the apostle was weak, tired, and lame from his journey. His feet were blistered raw and he didn't think he could go much farther without help. After considering the risks, he felt there was little choice. The settlement which he was approaching was familiar.

Hobbling to the cabin of some former church members, he found a familiar young man, who was happy to see the fugitive. The man told him that news of his escape had just reached the settlement. His friend took the fugitive on his own horse to his brother's cabin. These were staunch church members. The father was away, but the wife and children received Parker with joy. He relaxed and sat down to eat with them. Then a neighbor came to the door and things became tense. The neighbor was determined to wait for the man of the house, and the fugitive feared that when the father came home he would greet him by name.

Fortunately, as the father came up the path, his children went out and told him that Parker was there, just out of prison, and must not be exposed. When the father came in he and Parker did a good job pretending they didn't know each other. (Parker was a good actor by now!) The neighbor completed his errand and left, and the two friends greeted each other warmly. The man saddled his only horse for Parker and, running ahead of him and next to him, led him on his way. At midnight the man took back his horse and rode home. Parker was grateful for a full stomach and a chance to ride for awhile rather than walk.

His friend also told Parker about a different route to the Mississippi River and across it. This way would be more secluded and inconspicuous, (and therefore safer) than the one he had planned to take. Throughout the rest of the night Parker walked, so tired and stiff that he sometimes had to crawl on hands and knees until he limbered up.

Day dawned. Parker needed to get to a place where he could hide, but was so tired that he repeatedly fell asleep on his feet as he walked. Finally, finding a good hiding place, he slept until mid-day. Refreshed, he walked on.

Getting closer to home now, he was impatient. The apostle

calculated that if he did things right he would be able to reach the Mississippi by morning. Once across that, he was practically home. Impatient to be with his family in freedom once more, Parker began to take risks. He decided to do something new. In order to get to a town on his way, he walked through an open prairie in full daylight. The tired man decided that if he were found he would fight to the death rather than go back to prison.

About the middle of the plain, where the road turned, Parker suddenly saw two horsemen with rifles on their shoulders, too close to him for him to run. As soon as they both saw him they stopped, and one said. "There he is now." They started riding again toward him and he expected them to yell out his name at any moment. He knew if they did he'd grab their guns and overpower them or die. Miraculously, however, they passed him on the road, on either side of him, without saying or doing a thing!

Parker reached the small town and rejoiced, knowing he had only a few miles before "freedom" river. Finding what he thought was the path to the river, he struggled through the swampy "river bottoms" only to find that the small, muddy river was not the Mississippi. Gloomily he wondered how long he must keep going. It seemed to Parker that an "enchanted land" lay between him and his freedom. Would he ever be home again? Would he ever again rest?

Disappointed, Parker walked back to the town as the sun was setting, knowing that if he didn't reach the Mississippi during that night he'd be too disabled with hunger and fatigue to make it. He asked, and learned which direction he should take. He then spent that night fording rivers, walking, resting with a block of wood for a pillow, and finally reaching the Mississippi by dawn. He knew that once over the river and in Illinois, his enemies could harass him no more He also knew that they had every ferry watched, in order to make sure he didn't get across. As it became brighter and brighter the fugitive could see the "promised land"—Illinois—on the horizon.

This part was crucial. Parker could still lose everything if he were caught before he crossed the river. He prayed his thanks for past deliverance and fervently asked for help in crossing now. He then looked over the area, fortunately finding that no public ferries crossed at that town. He had some money with him, and so prevailed upon a boy to canoe him over the river, for which he paid well.

At last he was in Illinois, no longer either prisoner or fugitive, but legally a free man! He kissed the ground and fervently prayed his thanks. He had made it! He was almost home! He walked two miles toward Quincy before finding a house. He stopped to ask for food, and only a little boy was home. The boy gave him a pitcher of milk and he tried to drink only a little, enough to keep from fainting, but couldn't help himself and polished off the whole thing. Embarrassed, the fugitive waited for the mother to come in. She came up the doorstep and Parker recognized her as his former neighbor. She took one look at him, and screamed.

"Why, good Lord, is that you? All the world is hunting you—both friends and enemies; they had almost given you up!"

She ran around the kitchen, fixing him food and asking him question after question, also telling him all about the Saints and what everybody was doing. After feeding Parker, she took him out to her husband, who was working in the fields. Her husband dropped everything to help the apostle on his way, and led him through five miles of river bottoms toward Quincy. It was a hot, humid day. After a mile or two, Parker became overwhelmed with exhaustion and thirst. His friend let him lean on him and he talked to Parker: "Try to keep up a little longer, you're almost there; hang on." They reached a settlement. The apostle sat down in the shade and fainted. As he started to come to, he saw a man and his wife running toward him with cold water. His thirst was so unbearable that he tried to get up and run toward them for the quenching drink. Motioning to them to hurry, Parker staggered like a drunk and fell again.

The woman stopped running and said to her husband, "[This] cannot be [him], of whom I have heard so much—it must be some old drunkard." Her husband assured her that it was indeed the apostle, and they gave him sips to drink, until he felt better. In their home he bathed, shaved, borrowed clean clothes, ate and slept that night.

Now Parker was so close to home and he could hardly wait to see his wife and children, but was so weak that he needed to stay at that cabin and rest all day. At sunset he got on a horse and rode the twenty-five miles to Quincy and his wife, getting there about two in the morning. His wife had stayed up all night for four nights and most of the fifth, expecting his return, and had just about lost hope. Parker knocked at the door, she opened it and they held each other tight. Her dear husband, Parley Parker Pratt, was safe at last.

Morris Phelps escaped his pursuers and rode to Illinois safely before the ferries were watched and before any news had reached the area. He told the Saints that the three of them had escaped and everyone began watching for the other two.

King Follett was captured on his horse and put back in prison. Since he was not one of the church leaders, the men in the area soon started treating him better. They eventually laughed about what an adventure he had led them on and praised his bravery. Even so, he was imprisoned for several more months with that lovable duo, Luman and Phila, before he was released.

Mrs. Phelps' brother and Orson Pratt, the two accomplices, started to run but found they were surrounded on every side. They slipped into a ravine and lay still until the men had all left. They walked and reached Illinois soon after Mr. Phelps.

Mrs. Phelps, the third accomplice, was inside the prison when the men escaped. After they ran she was thrown outside and harassed and harangued in the public square, while men chased the escapees. A compassionate young man came and took her to his home, where his family protected her. She stayed with them while the mob "borrowed" her horse, on which they captured Mr. Follett. They searched for her husband, Morris, and Elder Pratt. After two weeks they returned her horse to her and she rode home to Illinois to her husband.

Parley P. Pratt was born April 12, 1807. He was made an apostle on February 21, 1835, when he was twenty-seven years old. He spent nearly all his life serving various missions and was murdered at age fifty.

Photo: *Parley P. Pratt*

.

Chapter Seven

NORA

Nora was born on a beautiful island in the Irish Sea, the Isle of Man, and raised in a religious home. Her father died at sea when she was a young woman, and because of the resulting financial problems in her family she went to London to serve as a "companion" to an upper-class lady.

In time she returned home and began working for the family of the governor of the Island. Nora had a good friend who was moving to Canada and the friend said she wouldn't go without Nora. Nora turned down the invitation. Then a dream convinced her that she should go to Canada, so she accepted.

On the trip across the Atlantic Nora was so sea-sick that she thought she would surely die then and there. Even so she felt well enough at times to hand out Methodist tracts. Nora kept a diary through this voyage and wrote about the landing at New York and her trip northward from there. She loved beauty and wrote about the natural wonders of the new land, always recording her thanks to God for his blessings. She also recorded her hopes that she could influence the family she accompanied to become more religious.

Once in Canada she began attending Methodist services, and became acquainted with the leader of her church class. He became more and more interested in this refined, gentle woman. Nora was a good conversationalist, attractive, witty, and intelligent, and religion was as important to her as it was to him. Yet she had no interest in him except as a friend, particularly since she was thirty-six years old and he was only twenty-four. The difference in ages didn't matter to him. He was in love and continued to court her. Finally he asked Nora to marry him. She turned him down flat. Then, once again she had a dream that would change the course of her life—it convinced her that she should marry her suitor. Always obedient to spiritual promptings, Nora accepted his proposal and they were married.

They both sought diligently for the true church. Within three-and-a-half years of their marriage they were converted and joined the Church. They gathered with the saints, suffering the persecutions that came.

In contrast to the life of wealth she had known with her English friends, poverty and loneliness were now Nora's lot. Her husband was called to serve a two-year mission in Great Britain. She and their children lived in a 20' by 20' room of a log building that had been a barracks. This was located in Montrose, Iowa (across the river from Nauvoo). The room was cold and drafty and the spaces between the logs let in more than just air: One winter a skunk came in every night, and they had occasional visits from a large snake. Drunken Indians tried to enter when she was up in the night with a sick child, but barracks neighbors kept them away. She and the children, along with most of the Saints there, struggled with malarial fevers and were almost constantly ill.

Meanwhile Nora's husband was preaching the gospel to her relatives and baptized her brother's family, including her nephew, George Q. Cannon, who later became an apostle. Her husband also went to her birthplace, the Isle of Man, and visited many of her girlhood friends, making some converts there. Nora enjoyed his encouraging letters during the mission.

Nora's husband returned to find her very sick. She had not written about this so he wouldn't worry. Alarmed, he called twenty other elders to her bedside and they administered to her. The administration was the turning point and she was healed.

Nora's husband built a two-story frame home in Nauvoo where he shortly moved her and their three children. Their lot provided room for a garden, as well as a barn to house animals. What a pleasant contrast to the log barracks! Yet now the sacrifices would be of a different nature. The Prophet Joseph Smith informed her husband that it was now time for the principle of plural marriage to be practiced.

Ever faithful, within two-and-a-half years Nora and her husband entered into the principle. They agreed that he would marry her first cousin, also born on the Isle of Man and baptized on the same day as she and her husband were baptized. As the years went on he also married others.

In Nauvoo, Nora waited fearfully as her husband was incarcerated with the prophet and others at Carthage Jail. She was terrified when she heard that Joseph and Hyrum had been killed. However, the message sent to Nauvoo said that her husband had only been injured, not seriously.

The second day after he'd been injured, Nora came with her father and mother-in-law to the town of Carthage to see her husband in the hotel where he was staying. She saw firsthand that his injuries were much more serious than he had indicated. He had signed the note to the Saints as quickly as he could, so his writing would be steady, not wanting to alarm her or to cause others to seek vengeance. A slug had lodged in his thigh, hit the bone and flattened. He was in a great deal of pain. When a doctor offered to remove it from his leg, he agreed and endured the operation without being tied down or having any form of anesthesia.

The hotel's owners openly approved of the murder of the prophet and Hyrum. During the operation Nora went into another room to pray for her husband, and while she was on her knees an old woman came into the room and patted her on the back. "There's a good lady, pray for God to forgive your sins; pray that you may be converted, and the Lord may have mercy on your soul!"

Militiamen guarded Nora's husband for the next few days as he recuperated, for there were mobbers who wanted to finish what they had begun, and to silence a witness. Finally several friends from Nauvoo came to take him home, even though he was so weak he could hardly talk. They carried him on a

litter until the jarring became too painful. Then they hitched a
sleigh to the back of a wagon and made a bed on it. Nora sat
by his side and administered ice-water to his wounds as the
sleigh moved smoothly over the tall prairie grass. Friends and
neighbors joined the group along the road to Nauvoo until it
became a procession.

Nora cared for her husband over the next weeks as he
gained strength. Because he was bedridden, in the next few
weeks church business meetings were held in their home. It
was also in her home that her husband, Elder Richards and
Elder Pratt met with Sidney Rigdon to deter him from pressing
his claims to church leadership. When they failed, they convinced him to at least wait until the other members of the
Twelve returned to Nauvoo.

Soon the majority of apostles had returned, including the
President of the Twelve, Brigham Young. The quorum met in
Nora's home to decide how to handle the situation of church
leadership. There they decided that Brigham Young would
speak for the Twelve at upcoming meetings. The next day the
church membership voted to sustain that quorum to lead the
church.

Again Nora was hostess to the apostles as they met repeatedly in her home to plan the church's future.

Finally Nora's husband recovered from his wounds, and
they went with the Saints to Utah. She lived for twenty more
years. However, Nora did not live to see her husband become
president of the church. Nor did Leonora Cannon Taylor see
the days when John Taylor, third church president, would be
personally persecuted because of polygamy. He lived out his
last days in hiding because of that principle.

Leonora Cannon Taylor was the wife of John Taylor, third president of
the Church. She was mother of three children who lived to adulthood.

Photo: *Leonora Cannon Taylor*

Chapter Eight
THE PRINCIPAL

F ew people can say they have taught school at Oxford. Oxford, Idaho, that is! In 1917 one young man was hired not only to teach there but to serve as the principal as well.

The eighteen-year-old taught the older students, surprised to find that some of them were older than he was. Worse, some of the boys were bigger! They saw their new leader as a challenge, and bragged that they would make things so miserable for him that he'd soon leave.

But the new principal was smarter than that. During lunchtimes he began teaching these boys to play basketball, and he even joined in and played with them. When they saw their new principal's athletic skills, their bad feelings turned into respect for him. Rather than being "kicked out," he stayed at Oxford school for three years, and was very popular with the students.

After the principal started playing basketball with the boys, they formed the Oxford Athletic Club, open to all men in the community. The young school principal played forward on the club basketball team, which played teams from neighboring towns. Play was so rough that he ended up with lifetime scars for souvenirs.

His involvement with teaching and athletics didn't dampen the principal's enthusiasm for another interest, music. While growing up he had taken piano lessons and also learned to play the cornet, the horns (alto, baritone, and French), and the organ. He enjoyed playing these instruments in several bands as a teenager.

Now, in addition to his other activities, the busy principal made time for music in his life. He played the piano for church and school, but wanted to do even more. In these early days of the century there was no TV, radio, or movies for entertainment and very little other diversion in the rural Idaho communities. The principal organized a group of ten young women into a chorus and they sang everywhere, in church, school and community events.

His musical involvement went further. Two brothers in town were organizing a dance orchestra and needed a trombonist. They asked the principal to join them. Although he had never played that instrument before he had played enough instruments to pick it up quickly.

Soon the dance band was playing "gigs" throughout a large area. They played the Charleston and other energetic new dances, as the "flappers" and their dates enjoyed themselves. At their peak of popularity the band played 2-3 times weekly, often performing a midweek dance as well as those on the weekends.

The dances often lasted into the early morning hours and required a lot of travel time. This often made it hard after a weeknight dance for the young principal to stay awake the next day in school. His parents, who farmed, needed the extra money he sent them from this second job, but they worried about his health during this busy time. One winter their worries were justified—he came down with pneumonia.

The principal's physical health wasn't the only reason his parents were concerned with the dance orchestra. They were aware of the drinking and partying that other band members and dancers participated in. As good Latter-day Saints, they worried about this. The principal later said that his parents "held their breaths" for him during this time, hoping he wouldn't be negatively influenced by the dance environment. He wasn't—their teachings and example held.

During the years at Oxford School, the young man taught school, was principal, taught and played basketball at school as well as on the community team, organized and trained the women's chorus, played in the dance band, served as Elder's Quorum President, and occasionally slept.

After three years at Oxford, the young principal left for a mission, and never again participated in sports, nor did he end up in a teaching career. He did, however, use his music for many years as he was organist for the weekly temple meetings of the Council of the Twelve. The pace he had set for himself at Oxford continued, and even increased during the rest of his life. The leadership skills he had exhibited at Oxford became more and more evident throughout his life. This man of many talents was Harold B. Lee.

Harold B. Lee was the eleventh Church president. He served nearly eighteen months, from July 7, 1972, to December 26, 1973. He was instrumental in initiating and implementing the church welfare plan and the church correlation program.

Photo: *Harold B. Lee*

Chapter Nine

JOSEPH

Joseph was a visionary man. He would not join any religion because of the "confusion and discord" that existed in the Christian religions of the day. He had many visions. One concerned the Tree of Life:

> I thought I was traveling in an open, desolate field, which appeared to be very barren.... Traveling a short distance further, I came to a narrow path. This path I entered, and when I had traveled a little way in it, I beheld a beautiful stream of water, which ran from the east to the west. Of this stream, I could see neither the source nor yet the mouth; but as far as my eyes could extend I could see a rope, running along the bank of it, about as high as a man could reach, and beyond me was a low, but very pleasant valley, in which stood a tree such as I had never seen before. It was exceedingly handsome, insomuch that I looked upon it with wonder and admiration. Its beautiful branches spread themselves somewhat like an umbrella, and it bore a kind of fruit, in shape much like a chestnut bur, and as white as snow, or, if possible, whiter. I gazed upon the same with considerable interest, and as I was doing so, the burs or shells commenced opening and shedding their particles, or the fruit which they contained, which was of dazzling whiteness. I drew near and began to eat of it, and I found it delicious beyond description. As I was eating, I said in my heart, 'I cannot eat this alone, I must bring my wife and children, that they may partake with me.' Accordingly, I went and brought my family...and we all commenced eating and praising God for this blessing. We were exceedingly happy, insomuch that our joy could not easily be expressed. While thus engaged, I beheld a spacious building standing opposite the valley which we were in, and it appeared to reach to the very heavens. It was full of doors and windows, and they were all filled with people,

who were very finely dressed. When these people observed us in the low valley, under the tree, they pointed the finger of scorn at us, and treated us with all manner of disrespect and contempt. But their [mocking] we utterly disregarded. I presently turned to my guide and inquired of him the meaning of the fruit that was so delicious. He told me it was the pure love of God, shed abroad in the hearts of all those who love him, and keep his commandments. He then commanded me to go and bring the rest of my children. I told him that we were all there. 'No,' he replied, 'look yonder, you have two more, and you must bring them also.' Upon raising my eyes, I saw two small children, standing some distance off. I immediately went to them, and brought them to the tree; upon which they commenced eating with the rest, and we all rejoiced together. The more we ate, the more we seemed to desire, until we even got down upon our knees and scooped it up, eating it by double handfuls. After feasting in this manner a short time, I asked my guide what was the meaning of the spacious building which I saw. He replied, 'It is Babylon, it is Babylon, and it must fall. The people in the doors and windows are the inhabitants thereof, who scorn and despise the Saints of God because of their humility.' I soon awoke, clapping my hands together for joy.

This was a remarkable vision, made all the more so because Lehi's vision of the tree of life had not yet been translated. In fact, at the time of this vision, the Book of Mormon translator was not even six years old! The "visionary" man was Joseph Smith, Senior, father of the prophet. Later, when the prophet Joseph had his early visions his father believed him implicitly. He had been prepared by revelations of his own in the preceding years.

Joseph Smith, Senior, was born July 12, 1771. He was the father of the prophet Joseph Smith and was made Church Patriarch as well as assistant counselor in the First Presidency. He died September 14, 1840, several years before his sons were martyred.

Photo: *Joseph Smith, Senior*

Chapter Ten

HARRY

The first nine years of Harry's life did not bode well for a happy future. He was born into an unstable home in England. Today we would call it dysfunctional. Harry's father was rarely home and spent most of his meager earnings on alcohol and gambling. He moved his family from place to place and then left his wife to fend for herself for months at a time.

Harry's mother was converted to the church and baptized soon after Harry's birth and her husband followed in order to please her. But his interest in the church soon waned, and the family's fortunes continued to decline.

Harry's mother had a great desire to join the Saints in Utah, and one day circumstances came about to make that possible. She received a letter from her husband which contained a rare, large sum of money. For once his gambling had paid off! He sent her the money in order that she might once again move and join him. But Harry's mother decided that this time, instead of continuing on this road leading nowhere, she would emigrate to Zion with that money. Unfortunately there was only enough for her to take two of her four children with her, so Harry and a sister were to stay behind. Harry's mother extracted a promise from the five-year-old boy that he would join her in Zion as soon as he was able. A heavy-hearted Harry watched as his mother's boat left for America.

Harry's sister went to live with relatives, but Harry's new home turned out to be a less fortunate choice. He went to live with a childless convert couple, the Toveys, and his life now went from bad to worse. In trouble with the law, the couple never stayed in one place for long. Like characters out of

Dickens, the poverty-stricken couple valued Harry only as he could contribute economically. He worked in their irregular stonemason business. He helped in their sometime bakery. He begged along with them during the summers, all around the region. At night he slept under tavern tables while they drank.

Then the inventive couple found a new way to exploit him: They turned his childish singing voice into a source of income. Now, rather than cower under the saloon tables every evening, Harry was made to stand on them and to sing vulgar, raucous songs to the accompaniment of his foster "father's" violin. Patrons threw coins, which were promptly spent on drink. Harry was never able to forget those songs with the off-color lyrics.

The boy was often hungry and cold, sleeping on the floor without any blanket, and was physically abused when the couple became drunk and violent. Yet, despite the horrors of his life, little Harry never forgot his mother's early religious teachings. Prayer was his solace.

When he was nearly nine the couple sent Harry away to a workhouse to apprentice as a shoemaker. His first night there, as Harry lay awake in the dark, a voice spoke to him. "If you are apprenticed to the shoemaker's trade tomorrow you will never see your mother in America." Remembering his promise to her, Harry ran away and spent weeks eating discarded food and sleeping wherever he could, trying to find the missionaries. Finally, his energy depleted, he returned to his foster "family." Once again they made plans to send him away, and once again he ran. Again he spent weeks on his own before he found the man he was seeking, whom he believed would safely harbor him. Instead the man returned him to the Toveys.

During those stark years one of Harry's greatest hungers was to learn to read. Neither his parents nor the Toveys could give him any schooling and his illiteracy was a constant source of pain. The Toveys did read to him from the Bible and L.D.S. writings (ironically). Despite his erratic life, Harry believed. He loved the sounds of words and longed to be able to read them himself.

One day Harry was traveling in the country with Mrs. Tovey and they sat down for a rest. Several pages of newspaper blew next to him and he begged her to read them to him. She began, but before long she fell asleep. In the quiet, Harry thought deeply about his lack. "Will the time ever come when books and papers will speak to me? Will I ever read books?" A voice answered him once again. "Aye, and you'll write them, too."

Not long after this, word came from Harry's mother in America that he was to board a ship and join her, courtesy of the Perpetual Emigration Fund. He crossed the ocean with his sister, and then together they crossed the plains to Utah. Harry lived again in his mother's home and received the education he so much desired. Later he would look back on his years in England and say, "My childhood was a nightmare; my boyhood a tragedy."

Many years went by and with the demands of life Harry forgot, for a time, the spiritual witness that he would write. Yet the voice proved to be prophetic. Harry became one of the most prolific writers the church has ever known. He edited the Millennial Star and wrote his own biography and those of the prophets he admired. Harry became the pre-eminent authority on LDS church history and doctrine of his day, writing many volumes of church doctrine and history. Despite the residual effects of his unhappy childhood, which never completely left him, B.H. (Brigham Henry) Roberts became a member of the Quorum of the Seventy. He was a powerful advocate for the truth both in his speaking and his writing.

B.H. Roberts was born March 13, 1857. He was made a member of the First Quorum of the Seventy when he was thirty-one years old. He wrote "Life of John Taylor," "A Comprehensive History of the Church," and many other theological, biographical and historical works.

Photo: *B. H. Roberts*

Chapter Eleven

THE PROPHET

Chase was never the prophet—he never became church president. But he had the gift to prophesy things that would come about in the future. Brigham Young called his good friend "my prophet."

Chase made a prediction concerning the Saint's future in Nauvoo. They had recently been driven from Far West, Missouri and were moving to Nauvoo in Illinois. Understandably, they hoped that Nauvoo would be the last place they would move. One day Chase was with a group of the brethren going up the Mississippi river to Iowa, to see about purchasing land on that side of the river as well. The men stood by the boat's railing on that fine spring day and admired the view of Nauvoo's location. Chase commented, "It is a very pretty place, but not a long abiding place for the Saints." Sidney Rigdon was upset by this comment, and irritably replied, "I should suppose that [he] had passed through sufferings and privations and mobbings and drivings enough to learn to prophesy good concerning Israel."

Chase, who had a good sense of humor, agreed with Elder Rigdon, and then said, "President Rigdon, I'll prophesy good concerning you all the time if you can get it!" His companions laughed. Five years later the martyrdom of Joseph and Hyrum occurred and less than seven years after the fateful prophecy was uttered the first Saints of the exodus left.

Chase was in the East on a mission to promote Joseph Smith as next president of the United States when the news of the martyrdom reached him. Once back in Nauvoo, he mourned with all the Saints in the city. It wasn't long before it became apparent that they would be forced once more to leave their beloved city to relocate far away in the unknown west. In 1845 Chase said, "I am glad the time for our Exodus is come...and although we leave all our fine houses and farms here, how long do you think it will be before we shall be better off than we are now? I will prophesy...that in five years, we will be as well again off as we are now." Indeed, after much privation they were settled and cities were once again established within five years.

Despite his penchant for hitting the mark in his prophecies, most people thought Chase had really blown it one time. This was in Utah, during the winter of 1848-49. The people suffered with cold and hunger as Chase predicted abundance soon to come. To his shivering listeners he said, "Never mind, boys, in less than one year there will be plenty of clothes and everything that we shall want sold at less than St. Louis prices." Prominent members of the audience loudly proclaimed their disbelief. Even Chase himself felt like he'd gone a little too far with that, considering it a "very improbable thing." As he sat back down he said to his brethren he was afraid he'd "missed it this time." Yet who could have foreseen the rush that would follow gold's discovery in California? From 15,000 to 20,000 "forty-niners" passed through Salt Lake City on their way to California in 1849.

The miners needed supplies, grain, and repairs to their wagons and harnesses. They bartered off their unneeded provisions, tools and clothes to lighten their loads. The Saints were able to trade at one-fifth to one-half the Eastern market value. Many Eastern merchants hurried goods to California overland, but hearing that others were getting them there in ships, feared they'd lose out and sold their goods cheaply in Utah. Who could have foreseen any of this?

In referring to this incident years later, Chase said,

> ...I have predicted things I did not foresee, and did not believe anybody else did, but I have said it, and it came to pass even more abundantly than I predicted...Nearly every man was

dressed in skins, and we were all poor, destitute and distressed, yet we all felt well. I said 'it will be but a little while, brethren, before you shall have food and raiment in abundance, and shall buy it cheaper than it can be bought in the cities of the United States.' I did not know there were any Gentiles coming here, I never thought of such a thing...but...it came to pass just as I had spoken it, only more abundantly. The Lord led me right, but I did not know it.

In 1853 Chase repeatedly counseled the Saints to store grain against a day of want, telling them it would be of more worth to them than gold and silver. He prophesied that they would see great sorrow if they failed to do this. For the next three years Chase emphasized this in all his sermons so that the people might be prepared. Sadly, most ignored the advice and suffered in the famine of 1856. Fortunately Chase had heeded his own advice, and by rationing his own family's food, was able to keep many others from starvation.

During this famine a man came to ask Chase's advice about finding food. Chase gave him some food and then told him to "go and marry a wife." The man thought that it would be foolish to marry when he couldn't provide food for himself. But recognizing the prophetic gift, the man decided to follow Chase's counsel. After thinking of a widow with several children who might marry him, he proposed and she accepted. She turned out to have a six month's supply of provisions!

When the U.S. Army moved troops into Camp Floyd, Chase prophesied that the United States would have to pay dearly for this move and for mistreating the church. His words proved prophetic. When the troops were withdrawn from the camp in 1861 (because of the Civil War) the Saints were the beneficiaries. The army was forced to auction off much of its equipment rather than move it. The Saints paid about $100,000 for equipment worth four million dollars.

In 1853 when the first cornerstone of the Salt Lake Temple was installed, Chase said that the powers of evil would rage and the Saints would be persecuted "when the walls reached the square." This was fulfilled fifteen years after his death. The walls "reached the square" (before the spires were added) in November 1882, eight months after Congress passed the "Edmunds Law" restricting polygamy.

Once a man who was working for him asked him for some "goods." Chase said no, and the man was angry. The man went home and prayed about it. The next morning when the man came to work, Chase asked him, "What have you been complaining to the Lord for...? Here are the things you asked me for, and after this don't go to the Lord about every little thing that happens."

We still quote today Chase's words which were only partially fulfilled, during the persecutions over polygamy:

> This church has before it many close places through which it will have to pass before the work of God is crowned with victory. To meet the difficulties that are coming, it will be necessary for you to have a knowledge of the truth of this work for yourselves. The difficulties will be of such a character that the man or woman who does not possess this personal knowledge or witness will fall. If you have not got the testimony, live right and call upon the Lord and cease not til you obtain it. If you do not you will not stand.
>
> ...The time will come when no man nor woman will be able to endure on borrowed light. Each will have to be guided by the light within himself. If you do not have it, how can you stand?

This man with the gift of prophecy was the first "President Kimball," Heber Chase Kimball.

Heber C. Kimball was a close friend of Brigham Young even before their mutual conversion to the gospel. He was ordained an apostle at age thirty-three and served as first counselor to Brigham Young for twenty years, until his death on June 22, 1868.

Photo: *Heber C. Kimball*

Chapter Twelve

THE STUDENT

The young mother sighed as she did her housework. It was the 1870s and she had no electricity or labor-saving devices to make her days easier. Sensitive, emotional, and intelligent, she wished that more of her time could be devoted to intellectual and spiritual pursuits. Why did she have to spend most of her energy and time each day in manual labor? Her formal education was limited, and she longed desperately for more. She looked at her three little barefoot boys and wondered what opportunities they might have for education and culture.

The woman's polygamous husband was a good man but he possessed no money-making talent. She and her three sister wives scrimped and worked for survival. There must be a better life; somehow she must find it. She resolved to study every morning early, from 4:00 to 7:00. Over the months she made progress, despite days and weeks of illness which prevented study time.

As a supplement to her personal study, she began taking nursing classes from a Salt Lake doctor. She had already lost two children. How could she better care for her remaining children so they could be strong and healthy? She enjoyed the nursing classes and began to think about Brother Brigham's statement that it was time for women to "come forth as doctors in these valleys of the mountains." Deep in her heart, this woman felt she had the aptitude and interest to become one of these doctors. Even Sister Eliza R. Snow had advised her to do so. If only there were a medical school nearby, she'd jump at the chance. But to go back East, leave her dear husband and boys for a period of years, was unthinkable.

Yet as the months passed this intelligent woman found herself pondering the unthinkable more and more. She knew that her husband, Bard, couldn't financially support them all. Her help would be needed. Becoming a doctor would combine all her goals. By magnifying her talents she would bless and save the lives of others, pave the way for a better life for her children, and help alleviate the financial burden in the family.

With Bard's full support she left to go to the Women's College of Medicine in Pennsylvania. As the train pulled away, she waved through her tears to Bard, eight-year-old Bard Junior, six-year-old Richie, and baby Burt, nearly fourteen months old. How she would miss them. How fortunate she was to have "sister wives" who could be surrogate mothers for them during her absence. Bard assured her the children would be well taken care of.

That first school year was difficult, with its long hours of study as well as dissecting in the cold lab. The student endured many moments of homesickness. Yet she loved learning about the human body; everything she learned served to strengthen her testimony of its Maker. Her particular emphasis was in maternal and child health. Her teachers were impressed with her mastery of the subject matter.

Summer came. Although the student missed her family, she knew that if she studied hard during the summer she would be that much farther ahead.

She took one break, however, when Bard came in June to visit her. They saw the sights of Philadelphia and relaxed and enjoyed each other's company. How she appreciated this welcome break from her studies!

Then bad news came. Her health had deteriorated. The doctors, and now Bard, insisted she return home for the rest of the summer to rest and recuperate. All her plans were upset. Yes, she would love to see her sons, but once home, would money and inclination ever let her return? Would all the sacrifices she and her family had made, to get one year of medical school finished, be in vain?

The student reluctantly left school to spend the summer with her family. She canned fruit, got to know her boys again, visited with sister wives, cleaned house. Always in the back of her mind—would she ever finish her schooling?

And then came the greatest shock of all—she was pregnant. Now certainly, there would be no way to finish school; her sacrifices had been in vain; her dream was gone. Her worst fears had come to pass, for this "temporary" visit home must become permanent.

After hours of pondering and prayer, the student decided that she would try to do the impossible—go back and finish. Her baby was due in May, after the end of the school term, and she would rely on the Lord to make this work. Her original reasons still stood: The dire need in the community, her need for a greater sphere of usefulness, and the ever-present, grinding need for money in the family. The lack of money was also an obstacle to her return. However, she knew the family must sacrifice now for opportunities later. If she didn't return now, when? It would never be any easier.

Again, the leave-taking was wrenching, more so as Bard, worried about her health, had mixed feelings this time.

The student once again left him and her boys. This time it would be a long eighteen months of absence. She thought her heart would break, but she had to do this.

In Philadelphia the student returned to her old boarding-house. Finances were a constant worry. She had enough money only to subsist on bread and milk, with bacon thrown in once in awhile. She studied until late each night in the library or dissecting room, in order to save money on heat and light for her room.

The doctors (who were also her teachers) were horrified when they learned of her expectant condition. They told her that she must have an abortion immediately because they feared her rigorous course of study would harm both her and her baby. After a night of earnest prayer, the student decided, "I came to learn how to save life, not to take it." She continued in her medical classes, never missing one. Her faith in the Lord and her precious letters from home were her sustenance.

Her baby girl timed her birth perfectly, coming during the medical school break. The student was given more comfortable lodgings for a few weeks, with a local family. This enabled her to rest and recuperate and enjoy her baby Olea. Then she returned to the grind of school, hiring a woman to take care of the baby in her boardinghouse.

All her hard work finally paid off. When Olea was ten months old, the student graduated and rode the train back to Utah. Ellis Reynolds Shipp had done the impossible: She was now an M.D.

Ellis R. Shipp became the second woman doctor in Utah. She not only had a private practice for the rest of her life, but taught classes in nursing and obstetrics to hundreds of LDS women. These, in turn, went home and served as midwives, teaching other women in their communities. Ellis herself delivered over 6,000 babies in her sixty-year medical practice.

Photo: *Ellis R. Shipp*

Chapter Thirteen
THE FISHERMAN

The year was 1892. "Forest and Stream" magazine published a letter by an eighty-five-year-old man, who enthusiastically recounted his fishing experiences of a lifetime. Because he had lived in so many different places, he had opportunities for a much greater variety of angling experiences than most people in those days could ever have.

The man had grown up in Connecticut and fished from the time he was old enough to hold a rod. This was more than just a recreational activity—it helped to feed the family!

As he grew up the man continued to love to fish. He became a farmer and was blessed with a hardy constitution, enjoying hard physical labor his whole life. But every so often even a hard worker needs a break, and he would often take it by going to a stream with his rod and reel.

At the age of thirty-eight the fisherman served as a mission president in England. There he learned to fly fish for the first time. His mentor was a seventy-year-old expert at his art. The student took several pages of his journal to describe the techniques and equipment used. Before leaving England he bought salmon and trout rods, reels, lines, hooks and flies for both salt and fresh water. He was now ready for some serious fishing!

He was a member of the 1847 vanguard pioneer company, and his skills came in handy as he provided needed sustenance for his fellow travelers. After helping to establish a settlement at Salt Lake City he once more crossed the plains, this time going East, to pick up his family at Winter Quarters. Once again he helped to provide fresh fish. In any group, he generally had the biggest catch. He happily noted that the fish always seemed to prefer his artificial fly to the lures others used.

Back in Winter Quarters, the fisherman was called to be the Eastern States mission president. While in Massachusetts he relaxed on a river bank with friends, catching most of the trout and pickerel they brought home for dinner.

After his mission he settled in Utah, always finding opportunities to go fishing. Whenever he went out of town he would pack his fly fishing gear and find a chance to use it. This relaxed him and helped him forget the many pressures of his life.

In his life this sportsman tried various Utah streams, in the days when fish were abundant and limits were unheard of. One day he caught forty-nine trout. Another time he and his father and a friend caught thirty-nine. Another day this trio caught 203!! They were pretty bushed at the end of that one.

While quite a purist in the use of the fly, the fisherman would occasionally use a net, like the time prior to a three-day conference in Provo, when he caught two bushels of fish from the Provo river in this manner. At other times, angling in the Provo river, he caught fish weighing as much as forty pounds.

The angler meticulously kept a daily diary most of his life, which is probably why he could write to a magazine near the end of his life with so many accurate details. He recorded his expeditions, numbers and kinds of fish caught, etc. But his penchant for recording detail yielded more than the minutiae of his own life; he also carefully recorded early church happenings and the talks of the brethren. His diary became the single most important source for early church history.

Who was this avid fisherman and journal-keeper? When his letter came out in "Forest and Stream" in 1892, he was the fourth president of the Church of Jesus Christ of Latter-day Saints. He had had the daunting task just two years earlier of issuing the Manifesto. By doing this he saved the church from the brink of destruction by its enemies. His name was Wilford Woodruff.

Wilford Woodruff was the fourth president of the Church. He served for over nine years, from April 7, 1889 to September 2, 1898. During his mission to England as a young apostle, he baptized hundreds of people in an eight month period. As a prophet he received the revelation (the Manifesto) which ended plural marriage. This lessened the severe persecution the Saints were enduring.

Photo: *Wilford Woodruff*

Chapter Fourteen

FAMILY SAGA

Jesus Christ foresaw that his doctrine would be such strong medicine that it would divide even close families. He said:

> Think not that I am come to send peace on earth: I came not to send peace, but a sword.
>
> For I am come to set a man at variance against his father, and the daughter against her mother, and the daughter in law against her mother in law.
>
> And a man's foes shall be they of his own household.
>
> He that loveth father or mother more than me is not worthy of me: and he that loveth son or daughter more than me is not worthy of me.

One family particularly exemplified this difficult reality.

They were an uncommonly religious family. The children were raised near the hamlet of Honidon, in England. The parents, like many of their neighbors, were "nonconformists," having left the Church of England to join another faith, in their case, Methodism. They did this because of their independence and freedom-loving spirit.

Eight children who lived to adulthood were born to these parents. They were: John, James, Thomas, Joseph, Ann, Mary, Martha, and Mercy. Each child would play his or her part in the family drama.

They were farmers, yet the children were also well-educated and taught the social graces. The father was a part-time Methodist preacher. Every Sabbath they all walked four miles, no matter the weather, to the chapel, unified by their strong faith. When James decided to study for the ministry, nothing could have made them all happier and prouder of him, for their faith was the most important thing in their lives.

When they became adults three members of the family decided to emigrate to the New World. Joseph and Mercy left first to farm in Canada and Mary followed two years later. These three must have been the adventurers of the family. Maybe the open-mindedness that led the parents to reject the state church also led the children to a faraway land. Maybe that same open-minded attitude permitted the children to accept a new religion when the opportunity came. In Canada the three were introduced to the gospel and within a very short time they knew it was true and were baptized.

Well-versed in the Bible, Joseph, Mary and Mercy knew that this new church contained the truths they'd grown up with and added much more. Rather than feeling disloyal to their family for having abandoned the faith, they probably felt they were being loyal to the spirit of what their parents had taught them: seek for truth and embrace it wherever it is found.

Within a year the three had left their Canadian farm and moved with the body of the Saints to Kirtland, Ohio. Mercy was by this time about thirty years old, Mary thirty-five, and Joseph still older, yet each remained unmarried.

The three soon took their separate paths. Mercy was soon married and went back to Canada on a mission with her husband. Joseph went to England on a mission, and after he'd gone Mary also was wed.

All the hopes of Mary and Mercy went with Joseph as he left for England. They hoped he would convert many people and particularly their five brothers and sisters. (Their parents were already deceased.) It had only taken the three of them days to recognize the truthfulness of the gospel. Certainly their religious-minded family members would recognize the truth just as naturally as they had done. To that end they had already introduced the gospel in letters to their brothers and sisters overseas.

Of all the siblings, James seemed the most promising

contact. He was considered the religious leader of the family. James was a Methodist minister who had initiated reforms within his faith, teaching his adherents to search earnestly for the original gospel. He shared the news of the gospel restoration with his flock, reading them his letters from Joseph, Mary, and Mercy. He asked his congregation to pray earnestly that the Lord would send missionaries from America to tell them more.

So it was with high hopes that Joseph visited James on his arrival in Preston, England. Their sister Martha and her minister husband were also there as Joseph talked about family news and finally about the gospel he'd come to preach. James was intrigued and invited Joseph to come back and visit that evening, and to bring his fellow missionaries. Joseph did so, and they talked late into the night. The atmosphere was cordial and warm. Martha was impressed with the gospel discussion and sent each missionary money the next day. James invited the missionaries to come and hear him preach the next day, Sunday.

After James' Sunday sermon he invited Joseph and the other missionaries to preach in his church that afternoon. He enjoyed their talks enough to invite them back that night, and then the next Wednesday night. James had prepared his congregation well for the new truths, and they were ready for everything the missionaries taught. As for Joseph and his companions, they were doing better than they could have dreamed. Prepared beforehand by James, many in his congregation already wanted to be baptized.

Suddenly James' attitude changed. These people were his flock and his own brother was taking them away. They were his stewardship as well as his livelihood! James refused to let the missionaries preach in his chapel any more, but it was too late. The people were interested and continued to invite the missionaries to preach in their homes. Only a week after their first address in James' chapel, the elders baptized nine people. James continued to lose people to the Mormons until nearly all his flock was gone. James had graciously invited Joseph to stay in his home, but now in his pride and hurt he angrily asked Joseph to leave. This was the beginning of the tragic family split. Though Joseph continued to labor in the same town, he saw James very little after that.

The brothers did keep writing, however. Each tried to convince the other that he was right. James never got over the humiliation of losing his congregation, and to his own brother! He became a powerful anti-Mormon speaker and writer, one of the church's strongest enemies in England.

Joseph wrote to Mary and Mercy to tell them what had happened, and they were very disappointed, having placed great hopes in their older brother's accepting the gospel.

Joseph now turned to his other siblings. He was assigned to labor in the Preston area and couldn't visit them personally, but wanted to share the gospel with them still. He wrote John, the oldest, but unfortunately, James had gotten to John first. John heartily resented Joseph for taking James' flock. John wrote to Joseph that he would only be welcome in John's home if he renounced his religion. In a long letter, John told Joseph that he loved Joseph and Mercy and Mary so much that it caused him to "deplore [their] misfortune...in being so much deceived [themselves], and being rendered so capable of deceiving others." John hoped that God would "keep [him] and the rest of the family steadfast and immovable in the true faith [Methodism]." Unfortunately, John died soon after this in an accident, before Joseph could talk to him in person.

Joseph sent missionaries to his sister Ann and her husband, who was a very influential minister. Ann's husband, like James, was initially very enthusiastic about the restored gospel. He invited the Elders to speak in his church several times. He even bore testimony to his congregation and asked them to be baptized. Then Ann's husband, like James, became very bitter against the church. He, too, became a very powerful enemy of the church in the several congregations he began throughout England.

Ann and her husband wrote many letters to Joseph to try and convince him of his delusion. They condemned Joseph and Mary and Mercy too, considering their conversion to Mormonism evidence that "if possible the very elect shall be deceived." Ann's minister husband wrote Joseph that the family offered many prayers for his deliverance.

Later Ann made a visit to Joseph in Preston. She talked with him and several other missionaries, and was favorably impressed, yet was never converted. Still believing him to be deluded, she nevertheless felt and acted more positively toward Joseph now. By the time he left England Ann even gave him and his wife several farewell gifts. (He'd married an Englishwoman.)

Joseph's brother Thomas was the most difficult sibling of all. When Joseph's mission duties finally permitted, he went to preach in the area where Thomas lived. Joseph stayed with Thomas initially but was treated so rudely that he had to find lodgings elsewhere. Thomas wouldn't listen to one word about Mormonism, nor would he let Joseph speak to his wife about it. Still Joseph preached in the area, and before he left he visited Thomas to say goodbye. As Joseph left Thomas' house for the last time they would ever see each other, Thomas called after him sarcastically over and over to beware of the Book of Mormon and that "Smith". Joseph left with regrets, and Thomas, like his brother and brother-in-law, became very publicly anti-Mormon.

Because of the strong personalities manifest in the members of this family, their rift influenced not only themselves, but the whole church. Joseph, Mary, and Mercy must have been not only hurt but embarrassed by their siblings. As a family biographer has said, "...[their family name] was synonymous with mounting opposition to the Mormon missionary effort in Great Britain...[their] kinsmen stood identified as the vanguard of anti-Mormon feeling..."

Their sister Martha alone was supportive. She, like Ann, was married to a minister. Though her husband was very much against the Mormons, Martha gave Joseph what help she could. She fed him, paid to have his laundry done, and gave him money. Martha always treated Joseph well and had good feelings toward the church, but she never joined.

Joseph visited his parents' gravesites while in England, and, perversely, was happy that they were deceased. He felt that if they had still been alive, they might have been influenced negatively toward the church by James and the other family members. Maybe it was better this way.

Joseph wrote Mary and Mercy regularly, but letters to them from antagonized family members became less and less frequent and then almost nonexistent. Still, wanting to keep a bond there, Mary named her daughter Martha Ann, after her two sisters in England.

Though he failed to baptize any of his own family, Joseph did a great work in the British mission. He preached, converted, baptized and presided there.

Joseph then returned to America. Eventually he and his wife, along with his widowed sisters, Mary and Mercy, crossed the plains to Utah together. Despite the pleadings of family members to renounce Mormonism, all three remained faithful through trials and persecutions that tested their faith to the utmost. The three demonstrated their commitment to their beliefs as they sacrificed their property, physical comforts and health for the Gospel's sake. Mary and Mercy, plural wives of the same husband, lost him in the persecutions that came. Had he lived, he could have supported them and eased the rugged path ahead for them and for his children. Joseph, Mary, and Mercy each remained faithful until their deaths.

Mary's testimony was, "The more I see of the dealing of our Heavenly Father with us as a people, the more I am constrained to rejoice that I was ever made acquainted with the everlasting covenant."

Mercy testified: "I would not now give up my religion for all the gold in America. I know I have not followed cunningly devised fables."

Mary died just a few years after coming to Utah. Joseph followed eleven years later. Mercy, the "baby" of the family, lived into her nineties. When Joseph and Mary had passed away she visited England.

Mercy hadn't seen her brothers and sisters for forty years. She visited James, Thomas and Ann. (Martha had passed away.) Mercy and Thomas visited the old Honidan homestead, Mercy looking wistfully upon the scenes of their childhood days. How close they had all been then, before the restored gospel had caused the family schism. Truly, "A man's foes [had been] they of his own household." Neither side ever came to understand the other.

Their family name was Fielding. Although none of Joseph's sons grew to maturity, preserving the family name in the church, it has been preserved in the names of the son and grandson of Mary Fielding Smith. Her son and grandson were both prophets: Joseph F. (for Fielding) Smith and his son, Joseph Fielding Smith.

Mary's biographer noted: "Perhaps the heart of no family was wrung so hard as that of the Fieldings by an issue, both sides manifesting sincere conviction."

Joseph Fielding served as a missionary in Great Britain for over four years. Over two years of this was spent as the second British Mission President.

Mary Fielding Smith was the widow of Hyrum Smith.

Mercy Fielding Thompson also became a plural wife of Hyrum after the death of her first husband.

Photo Top: *Joseph Fielding*
Photo Bottom Left: *Mary Fielding (Smith)*
Photo Bottom Right: *Mercy Fielding (Thompson)*

Chapter Fifteen
GOTTFRIED

Gottfried was a European convert to the church. A teacher by profession, in his own country he could have made a good living. However, he had gathered with the Saints to Utah and was finding it difficult to earn enough to feed his family.

In his own country he would have been paid a salary. In Salt Lake City in the early 1860s he discovered that people used the barter system, paying him in goods. Gottfried worked hard, teaching by day with a night session as well, cleaning up the school after hours, and traveling around the community lecturing on the side. Yet people couldn't afford to pay him what he was worth. The proud man sometimes had to take his wheelbarrow around the neighborhood and ask people to "pay up." Sometimes he came home with an empty wheelbarrow: His student's families were as poor as his own. He forgave them.

Not only was his standard of living lower in Utah than it had been in Europe, so was Gottfried's prestige in the community. Salt Lake City was still a frontier town, and because so many had to struggle to eke out a living they looked down on those who made their living with the head instead of the hands. They couldn't see the importance of education when they had to work so hard for subsistence. Because of this, many didn't feel obligated to help support him. They felt, "If he's too lazy to work for a living, let him starve."

Seeing his family go hungry made Gottfried resort to measures that the proud man would never have considered otherwise. At a party once, when all was quiet, he told the gathering, "If any of you have anything you do not care for, [I] will be glad for something to eat."

Full of faith, he prayed earnestly to his Heavenly Father for relief. One day a letter came that seemed to be the answer to all his prayers.

The letter was from his father in the "old country." He pleaded with his teacher son to come home and leave the Mormons who were so poorly regarded. His father promised Gottfried that money and position and the respect of all in his community would again be his, as they had been before he left, if he would only return. The teacher remembered how much different things had been for him before his conversion. His profession was respected back home. In it he had never faced want or derision.

In his poverty Gottfried pondered what course of action to take. Was his father's invitation his answer? Then one night Gottfried had a dream:

> It seemed to him that he could see a very steep mountain ahead which he must climb. When he looked for a path, he found none, and wondered how he would ever be able to accomplish the task before him. With much effort, however, he was able to climb step by step up the steep incline until he reached the top. There he beheld a landscape beautiful beyond description, and a smooth road with an even grade. When he awoke, he knew this was the answer to the question which had been troubling him.

Gottfried knew from this dream that hard times wouldn't be his lot always, and that assurance gave him the strength to endure. He arose from the dream and threw the tempting letter from his father into the fire. Then Gottfried fell to his knees, praying his thanks. He reflected:

> If it had not been for the testimony of the Gospel of Jesus Christ of Latter-day Saints, I should long ago have been back in my native land. [However] I would rather have suffered the afflictions of Job...than to have yielded to the enticements of

my...kinsmen and pseudo friends. I would rather take my wheel-barrow and go day by day among this people, collecting chips and whetstones for my pay, then to have the Kingdom of Saxony open to me, if such meant the sacrifice of my knowledge and testimony of this Gospel.

In time, word of Gottfried's capability as a teacher came to Brigham Young, and the prophet hired him as a private tutor to his own children. From then on, though he never became wealthy, Karl Gottfried Maeser was financially secure.

Karl G. Maeser was the first principal of the Brigham Young Academy and served from 1876 to 1888, when he became General Superintendent of all Church schools. Through his influence many students not only learned the "3 Rs", but grew in their testimonies of the gospel. He was loved and revered by his students.

Photo: *Karl G. Maeser*

Chapter Sixteen

THE VISITOR

Church services had already begun at the Central Baptist church in Moscow that rainy, gray, fall day. Few young people went to church. Church-goers were persecuted by the state, so most of the worshippers were middle-aged and elderly. Unexpectedly the services were interrupted as a group of Americans entered the building. The Muscovites stared, open-mouthed. In those Cold War days Americans rarely were allowed in the country. But here were Americans attending Christian services. As the foreigners walked down the aisles to be seated, men and women reached out to touch their hands, even to grasp them.

Everyone was curious about the exotic Americans, and the minister invited their leader to speak. Would he dare do so, here in the shadow of the Kremlin? The tall man with an obvious air of authority, turned to his wife, and with her nod of encouragement, stepped to the podium. He looked around at the anxious, yet hopeful faces. He began to speak, a Russian man from his group translating. The audience hung on his every word, and as he began to speak about faith, hope, and love, the people wept. He spoke about the Savior and the reality of eternal life.

"Our Heavenly Father is not far away. He is our Father. Jesus Christ, the Redeemer of the World, watches over this earth...Be unafraid, keep His commandments, love one another, pray for peace, and all will be well. This life is only a part of eternity. We lived before we came here...We will live again after we leave this life...I believe very firmly in prayer. I know it is possible to reach out and tap that Unseen Power which gives us strength and such an anchor in time of need. I leave you my witness...that truth will endure. Time is on the side of truth. God bless you and keep you all the days of your life."

Tears fell from the face of the speaker, as well as his listeners. Reluctantly he and his group moved slowly down the aisle since they had to catch a plane. Russian believers waved handkerchiefs and gripped the visitors' hands, and then began to sing together in their beautiful tongue, "God Be With You Till We Meet Again." Their faith in God was almost palpable, as was their love for his servant who had just spoken to them. The Spirit of the Lord confirmed to them that, despite their present circumstances, the Lord did love and remember each of them.

As the Americans slipped back into their cars they were all crying, even those hardened reporters in the group who had been avowed cynics about religious matters. When they arrived at the airport they crowded around the speaker. Many told him they'd just had the greatest spiritual experience of their lives.

As the speaker had said, time would indeed be on the side of truth. Yet it would be thirty years before the Russian people could begin once more to worship without retribution. There was a prophet presiding over the Church of Jesus Christ of Latter Day Saints when the winds of freedom began to blow again in Russia. He was the American who had spoken so movingly that day of God's love for his children everywhere: President Ezra Taft Benson.

Ezra Taft Benson was the thirteenth president of the Church. He served for eight-and-a-half years, from November 10, 1985, until his death on May 30, 1994. During his apostleship he served as Secretary of Agriculture under U.S. President Eisenhower. It was in this capacity that he visited the Soviet Union. His Church Presidency was marked by his emphasis on the Book of Mormon.

Photo: *Ezra Taft Benson*

Chapter Seventeen

INDOMITABLE LADY

S he was plucky. No matter how tough things got, she refused to give up.

Finances were always a problem for her frontier family. They worked hard but luck was often against them. As farmers, they were subject to the vicissitudes of nature and had other misfortunes as well. Medical bills for a child were the latest obstacle to security. The woman's family moved to Norwich, Vermont, hoping that the farm they rented there would be more productive, the weather would be better, and they might finally prosper.

Along with farming they added a business to try to insure their success this time. It was a "cake and beer" business, operated out of their home. They sold root beer, cakes, gingerbread, fruit and boiled eggs, as well as their handmade baskets and brooms. She learned to paint oil tablecloths and sold those, too. Everyone in the family, including the youngest children, pitched in to help however they could.

Notwithstanding all their effort, after two seasons of crop failure they decided, if there was a third, they would move on to greener pastures once more. The third summer was cold and they decided to move west.

The woman's husband left to find a suitable farm, while she stayed behind to make preparations to move. A neighbor, Mr. Howard, planned to go to the same area that fall, so she paid him to let her and her eight children go with him. The determined woman was ready for anything. She packed all her household goods and clothing, with her mother's and older sons' help, and they were on their way. By the time they left that fall it was already cold and snowy.

They went by sleigh for the first few miles and dropped off her mother at a relative's home. Then they put their belongings in a wagon for the remainder of the three-hundred-mile trip. Mr. Howard drove the wagon and the family walked, apparently with another family that was also moving. To her surprise, she "discovered that Mr. Howard, [their] teamster, was an unprincipled and unfeeling wretch." The woman's ten-year-old son, after three years on crutches, had just stopped using them and was still lame. Yet the driver often refused to let the boy ride on the wagon. Mr. Howard made him walk for miles at a time, as he preferred to let the girls in the other family ride next to him. Understandably, this made the woman's older sons very angry, and when they tried to intervene, the man knocked them down with the butt of his whip.

The woman gritted her teeth to endure whatever was necessary. They would soon be through with this cruel man. Then, about one hundred miles from their new home, came the last straw. Her eighteen-year-old son came to her with the news that the teamster had dumped all their belongings in the road and was taking off with her team. After finding the man in a barroom, she confronted him in front of all the travelers, demanding to know why he'd abrogated their agreement to take her things to their destination and stolen her horses. He replied that he had used up all her money and could take her no further.

She then turned to the audience in the barroom. "Gentlemen and ladies, please give your attention for a moment. Now, as sure as there is a God in heaven, that team, as well as the goods, belong to my husband, and this man intends to take them from me, or at least the team, leaving me with eight children, without the means of proceeding on my journey."

The courageous woman then turned to the man himself, and said, "Sir, I now forbid you touching the team, or driving it one step further. You can go about your own business; I have no use for you. I shall take charge of the team myself, and hereafter attend to my own affairs." As he tried to drive off, she grabbed the reins and the children got on the wagon, pushed him off, and they drove away as the bar patrons cheered them on.

Continuing her trip, the woman paid innkeepers along the way with cloth and clothing. By the time they met her husband in their new town, they were destitute, with little left of either cash or goods.

Yet their move turned out to be propitious; they did better in their new home. Once again they sold her oil tablecloths and food, and her husband and sons did manual labor jobs as well. Within two years they had enough to buy a farm, where they cleared the land, planted crops, and built a log house. They sold ashes from the burnt trees for making soap, sold firewood, and made and sold maple sugar, as well as the foods and wares they had previously made and sold. Fishing, hunting, and trapping further supplied their needs. Finally they were more than surviving, and made friends who admired and liked them for their hard work and trustworthiness.

The move proved to be blessed in another respect, as well. It put them in close proximity to a hill called Cumorah. This hill would figure prominently in her life and the lives of the entire family. Three-and-a-half years later her son Joseph (who had been lame on the journey) walked into the woods to pray. This "walk" changed their lives forever. In contrast to the high esteem in which their neighbors had held them, her family was vilified and persecuted. Yet no matter her circumstances, Lucy Mack Smith always showed courage, faith and pluck.

Lucy Mack Smith, mother of the Prophet Joseph Smith, was born on July 8, 1776. She bore eleven children and raised nine of them, and was a stalwart in the church. After the deaths of her sons Joseph, Hyrum, and Samuel (who also died as a martyr soon after his brothers), she chose not to go west with the Saints. Due to her age and poor health she stayed in Nauvoo and died May 5, 1855, at age seventy-nine.

Photo: *Lucy Mack Smith*

Chapter Eighteen

THE PASTOR AND HIS FRIEND

The man walked, head bowed. He had a lot on his mind. Thousands of miles from his congregation in New York, he strolled the streets of Salt Lake City. The minister had come to Utah to speak. Famous for his affirmative outlook, he wanted to encourage those who were downhearted and to lift them. He had spoken all over the United States. Yet this time, despite all the principles he taught and practiced, he himself needed lifting. He grappled with a problem that, no matter how he turned it around in his mind, seemed to defy solution. Peace eluded him.

The pastor's friend had invited him to meet the LDS Church Presidency. This clergyman had met other presidents, but not the current one. As he walked to the meeting he was preoccupied with his inner concerns and he prayed silently for guidance.

As he was ushered into the church presidency's office, the pastor was pleased with the cordiality of these men. A very spiritual man himself, he felt that he was a good judge of character. He felt that these men were certainly men of God. The time went quickly and pleasantly for the pastor as they visited. At the close of the conversation he realized how close he felt to the church president, who had been a stranger just moments before. He sensed what a deeply spiritual man this was, how deeply loving and concerned for others. Suddenly he wanted to reach out to him and seek the help he needed at that time.

"President, will you bless me?"

The prophet may have been startled, but if so he didn't show it.

"You mean you want me to give you a blessing such as I

give our people?"

"Yes."

"Certainly."

The prophet of God came around behind his new friend. He and his counselors placed their hands upon the man's head. In his quiet, sincere, loving manner, the prophet gave the pastor a blessing. He asked the Lord to bless this good man, to be near him and love him and take care of him, to guide him. During the blessing the pastor became very touched and felt of the Spirit of God. Tension was replaced with tears. Peace came. He knew he was known by name to his Father and his prayers had been heard.

The minister thanked his new friends. Goodbyes were said, and the pastor walked back onto the same street, feeling much differently. This time he could enjoy the sunshine and the snow-covered mountains. The answer then came and he knew what he needed to do to resolve the difficulty. The burden was lifted. Once more, his faith was renewed.

The pastor was Norman Vincent Peale; the prophet, President Spencer W. Kimball.

Spencer W. Kimball was the twelfth Church President. He served for nearly twelve years, from Dec. 30, 1978, until his death on Nov. 5, 1985. His presidency was marked by many church organizational changes and by the revelation granting the Priesthood to all worthy males.

The Reverend Norman Vincent Peale wrote more than forty-six books, including "The Power of Positive Thinking." He preached a practical Christianity in which people could use faith and prayer to solve their problems.

Photos: *Spencer W. Kimball, Norman Vincent Peale*

Chapter Nineteen
LUCY'S FRIEND

L ucy had a friend. He had loved her from the time he first knew her, when they were both children. At her mother's death, Lucy had come to live with her paternal grandparents, President and Sister Wilford Woodruff. Her friend lived near the Woodruffs. As a mischievous boy, he could only show his admiration toward Lucy by teasing and harassing her. This didn't win many points from the object of his adoration.

At age twelve the boy went away to the Brigham Young Academy for a year. He had changed a lot when he returned home as a thirteen-year-old. Now he was a young gentleman and continued to woo Lucy. One day he carried groceries home for her, then doffed his hat to her as he left. Lucy told her grandmother, "I just met [my friend]...He's home from school, and he's decent!"

Yet Lucy's friend had rivals. The scales weren't balanced very evenly, either, for his competitors for Lucy's attention come from wealthy families. They had the money and time to participate with Lucy in a variety of fun activities. This friend, on the other hand, was a member of a large polygamous family. His father was a church leader and had little extra time or money. How could the boy compete? He couldn't even stay in school because of family finances, but had to work to help the family stay afloat while his father was on his mission.

Despite his seeming handicaps, Lucy's admirer had a competitive nature and wanted to be the best at everything he did, whether at his menial labor jobs or at impressing Lucy. While members of the "in" group were having lawn parties on their well-groomed grass, he lived in a rundown house complete with a dirt yard. Yet he wanted to fit in. So while his father was away on a mission, the boy and his mother seeded their lawn. He carried water every night from an irrigation ditch to help it take root. Eventually he, too, was holding the coveted lawn party with Lucy and her friends.

When his father returned from his mission, Lucy's friend went to a local school. Then, again in need of money, he went to work on the railroad. His eyes were damaged as he worked on a railroad survey crew in the hot sun. He was never again able to see well enough for schooling.

The time came when her admirer's rivals for Lucy's affections narrowed down to just one. Even though her friend was competitive, he could never hope to court Lucy on the same level as this wealthy suitor. His rival had not only the money, but the time, to lavish on Lucy. This suitor seemed to have everything: looks, charm, and class.

Her friend, meanwhile, was working out of town as a traveling salesman. He had a loud, plaid suit, bow tie and wide-brimmed hat, in which he did comedy routines along the way. He entertained not only his partner, but others in the groups of traveling salesmen they met in small hotels along their route. He played the Jew's harp, guitar and harmonica and sang funny songs in his routine.

Maybe the comic routine helped to compensate in part for missing Lucy. While the young man was on the road for months, his wealthy rival wasn't wasting time at home. Lucy was fickle in her affections, preferring whichever young man was currently present. Now that her neighbor was away for so long, their relationship hit a new low. Even so, where there's mail, there's hope, and Lucy did continue to write to him.

When he was twenty-one the young man was called to serve a two-and-a-half-month mission to reactivate young men and women in outlying areas of Utah. Again his comic routines lightened the way. At one stop a family laughed so hard at him that he had to stop before the woman fainted! Yet again his outer humor belied his inner unhappiness, because at this time things came to a head with Lucy.

Her other beau was pressuring her to marry him and she became almost ill over what to do. Her absent friend even learned that Lucy was planning her marriage to the other man. Her friend refused to pressure her as his rival did, sincerely putting her happiness first. He had her picture with him on his short mission, and wrote to her:

> [Your picture] recalled to me a time when I never knew what it was to be jealous; but it was a long time ago. I then thought that I could live for you and you for me, and we would always be happy. But it seems that such a thing was not to be, and maybe it is better so...Be prayerful and humble; do not mistake the duty you owe to others. Your first duty is to yourself. I feel that you will be happy and my prayer is that you will.

Lucy stopped her wedding plans, maybe to wait until he returned and she could make a fair decision. Yet even when he came home Lucy vacillated in her feelings. Finally she wrote a letter to the other man telling him that she would marry her longtime friend. Even so, she wrote in her diary that day, "I mailed my decision and wished my heart was more at rest."

The other man must have been extremely persistent for he still would not give up. Lucy continued to see him for the next few months. Then came an event that forced her decision: Her friend, now her fiancee, got a two-year mission call to the Southern States. He felt they needed to resolve this before he left, so he could concentrate fully on his mission. He issued her an ultimatum:

> I will not encourage you any more, but will wait until you are strong again, and more able to realize the love I bear for you. When you, if ever, can come to me and tell me that you are not encouraging [the other man], then can I feel that I am free to hope for your love without doing anyone on earth an injustice.

So Lucy made her decision once and for all: It would be her old friend. Within the month they were married. Her short time to prepare for her wedding was complicated by her other suitor's response to her decision: He demanded that she return all his gifts and said he would move far away and never come back alive. She worried about his implied threat to commit suicide. Yet after her husband had gone to Tennessee on his mission, while Lucy prepared to join him, the other man returned to town to see Lucy again. Before long, however, she was in Tennessee where she served the rest of his mission with her husband.

Though Lucy truly loved her husband, she wondered for a time if she had made the right decision. It wasn't until years later (when she saw the way her former boyfriend had turned out), that her judgment was fully vindicated. Lucy would tell her children over and over through the years, "I nearly made a terrible mistake."

Time proved Lucy's judgment to be sound. Her husband possessed all the qualities that were most important to Lucy. In their twelfth year of marriage he was called as an apostle. On May 21, 1945, George Albert Smith became the eighth president of the church.

George Albert Smith became Church President May 21, 1945 and served nearly six years until his death on April 4, 1951. He and Lucy were married over forty-five years and had three children. President Smith was known as a loving, kind man and sent help to European Church Members who had suffered much during World War II.

Photos: *George Albert Smith, Lucy Woodruff*

Chapter Twenty
SHARING CULTURE

This was an unlikely place to "get culture," a 15' X 30' log cabin in the temporary community of Mt. Pisgah, Iowa (between Nauvoo and Winter Quarters). Both cabin floor and roof were made of dirt. The presiding elder of Mt. Pisgah, owner of the cabin, was deeply concerned over their primitive living conditions, the poverty, sickness and death which were a part of their everyday life. He reasoned, these people need some entertainment. Particularly under these conditions.

This wasn't the first time this man had tried to lift others' sights above the mundane. He had taught school and had taken great pride in teaching a class of students with "mentally dormant brain[s], ... elevat[ing his] students to a higher standard of intellectual improvement." He was successful in doing so, and won much praise because his students had progressed so far under his tutelage.

The Elder's living conditions contrasted sharply with the wealth of his parents' estate in Ohio. There he had participated in many evenings of entertainment, in an elegant hall reserved for such. Though his parents taught him to work hard, they also considered fun and recreation to be important. He knew the value to the human spirit of having productive leisure time, of balancing work and drudgery with fun. The principle was the same, regardless of the elegance or lack of it, in one's surroundings.

So here at Mt. Pisgah, in his primitive cabin, the elder had his wives cover the log walls with sheets, put clean straw on the floor, hollow out turnips to use as candle holders, and they threw a party. Guests participated in an evening of entertainment "as we served up a dish of succotash, composed of short speeches, full of life and sentiment, spiced with enthusiasm, appropriate songs, recitations, toasts, [riddles], exhortations, etc. At the close, all seemed perfectly satisfied, and withdrew, feeling as happy as though they were not homeless." This was one of many get-togethers at Mt. Pisgah, usually in the presiding Elder's cabin, when he initiated opportunities for recreation to lift people's spirits.

He was one of the few pioneers who had been to college, even though for only one term. Still, that made him one of the best educated of any. Not only did he love to learn and improve himself, he was blessed with an understanding of the needs of others for recreation and stimulation and had an ability to help provide it. In this he was fully supported by his leader, Brigham Young, who believed that "Recreation and diversion are as necessary to our well-being as the more serious pursuits of life."

When the leader left Mt. Pisgah and arrived in Utah, he built a nine-room adobe house for his large family. Then he began having "soirees" in his home. He decided to give their meetings a fancy name—The Polysophical Society, which one member translated to mean: "Many Sciences." The group of friends met every week or two on Wednesdays in the leader's home to entertain and enlighten each other. Though they were isolated in the "wilderness" of Utah, they could still experience some culture to soften the practical aspects of daily life.

Members of the group had several instruments on which they took turns playing in the meetings, including string instruments, a bagpipe, flute, piano and clarinet. Some members treated the group to vocal selections. Sometimes the group learned about the Deseret Alphabet, or had essays read to them. Sometimes they told jokes. A noted poetess often read her latest effort to the appreciative group. Some of the presentations were even given in foreign languages. The goal was for everything to be uplifting and refining as well as entertaining.

Each part on the program was assigned beforehand so everyone could be well-prepared, but no one was told in what order he would present his part. This kept everyone on their toes. One of the host's children would notify each participant with a note when he or she was next, and each part was to go no longer than fifteen minutes (their leader wanted to keep things moving). The meetings finally outgrew one home, and they began meeting at the Social Hall. The group soon had to go on without its genial instigator, because he was called to preside in Box Elder.

In Box Elder he was again a pioneer, starting over in a barren, new country. He renamed the town Brigham City, after the prophet. True to form, he hardly had the bare essentials of survival accomplished before he began again to combine recreation, socializing, and learning, to brighten the people's lives. The presiding Elder hosted skits, parties, and lectures in his home. When the courthouse was begun, he started the Dramatic Association of Brigham City in its basement. When the props and costumes were ruined in a destructive wind, he instigated construction of a new home for the dramatic society. The plays performed there were reportedly the best in the territory, next to Salt Lake City.

Not only did this leader seek to meet the people's spiritual, intellectual and recreational needs, he planned to better their material situation as well. Although his ideas were based on the United Order revealed to Joseph Smith, they were new and innovative. He instituted the cooperatives in Brigham City, with an umbrella name of the Brigham City Mercantile and Manufacturing Association. His goal was "to furnish every person employment, wishing to work; and pay as high wages as possible—mostly in home products." The community became essentially self-reliant under his leadership.

Under his plan, Brigham City boasted a tannery, woolen factory, silk and cotton industries, several farms, dairies, sawmills, a woodworking factory, and many other departments, forty in all. He succeeded in making the city so prosperous that when other Utah cities began cooperatives they patterned theirs after the Brigham City model.

Late in life, at age seventy-two, this leader was imprisoned for practicing plural marriage. Committed to "improving each moment" of his eleven-month stay, he held church meetings and, with others, held a school for other "co-habs" (Mormon polygamist inmates). In this school the men studied the gospel, math, bookkeeping, reading and writing. He also helped organize many other activities to keep them all busy through the long, dark and dank prison days.

Always, his desire was to improve the common lot and bring a higher standard of living to his people in every way. He wanted them to be happier and more fulfilled in this life, as well as the next. He believed that "A religion or system is of very little account, where it possesses no virtue nor power to better the condition of people, spiritually, intellectually, morally and physically." Few men had the organizational and creative abilities he did which enabled him to bring this about in people's lives.

Who was this innovator? He was Lorenzo Snow, who later became fifth church president.

Lorenzo Snow became Church President September 13, 1898. He served three years until his death October 10, 1901. During his administration the law of tithing was given new emphasis, restoring financial prosperity to the Church.

Photo: *Lorenzo Snow*

Chapter Twenty-One
A JAIL VISIT

Mary wed quite late in life: She was thirty-six and her husband, thirty-seven years old. Since her husband was a widower with five children, she had assumed the responsibilities of motherhood immediately upon her marriage. Soon she was expecting a baby and was happy about it, for this child would be their very own. Yet this baby, if she could have foreseen it, would be born in the very worst of times.

They lived in Far West, Missouri that fall of 1838. Mob violence increased day by day until it reached fever pitch. Armed men imprisoned her husband and several others on a cold November day. The prisoners were to be executed the next morning. Fortunately General Doniphan intervened and the execution didn't take place; however, the prisoners were taken to the jail at Richmond and then Liberty, Missouri.

Mary was heartsick. Her baby was due any day. She needed her husband by her side more than at any other time and he couldn't be with her. She didn't even know from day to day whether he was alive. Just days after his arrest, she had her baby, a boy.

Mary had long anticipated having this child, but she could never have imagined it would be under these circumstances. Mobs were everywhere, raping, murdering and looting as the Saints prepared to leave for Illinois. A group of them burst into her defenseless home, ransacking and taking almost everything she owned. Her baby was nearly suffocated in the struggle.

Refugees from surrounding communities straggled into Far West, making it necessary for the citizens to share their meager food. Mobbers ruined the Saints' cornfields. Nourishing food was hard to find. It wasn't safe to leave town to get food.

The young, underfed mother caught cold. Then a fever prevented her from getting back on her feet. The drafty house in which she lived only made it worse, and weeks spent in bed turned into months. Her sister, who had a baby as well, nursed Mary's baby for her and cared for the other five children. An older man and woman who lived with the family also helped.

Mary's husband languished in his bleak dungeon, unable to help in any way. He desperately wanted to see his wife and son, so he wrote, asking her to come. Mary may have felt he was asking the impossible, but she also knew that soon she would be moving 200 miles away (to Quincy, Illinois) and would be unable to visit him at all. And this might be their last visit. Many still wanted him killed.

So Mary decided, despite her circumstances, to go to him. It was a bitter cold February day when the new mother lay down on a bed in a wagon with her eleven-week-old baby. Her husband's brother drove the wagon and her sister came along with her own baby to care for the new one. Also Mary's sister-in-law came, bringing her son, to visit her husband who was also imprisoned.

They had forty miles of rough roads to travel, not only facing the extreme February cold, but the threat of mob harassment along the way as well. After two long, cold days of travel, they arrived safely at the Liberty Jail. The weak mother walked into the foul, dark dungeon with her baby. Mary rejoiced to see her husband alive. The group spent the night visiting and admiring the two babies. She was thankful she could be there in spite of her illness. How she had missed her husband these three months! Even though it was wonderful to be with him and see his joy in their baby, she couldn't bear to observe the loathsome conditions under which he was forced to live. Morning came and again she lay in the wagon for the trip home, relieved that the purpose of their visit was accomplished.

Just a few days later Mary was again lying in a cold wagon, this time for the long trip to Illinois. By the end of

February she was safely in Quincy. Once there she was sustained with good food. Able to rest free from worry about mobs, she began to regain her health. By the time her husband joined her in April, she was able to take care of him and help him recover his own health.

This woman who made the winter trek to Liberty Jail was Mary Fielding Smith, wife of Hyrum. The new baby she took to show him was Joseph F. Smith.

Mary Fielding Smith was sister to Joseph Fielding, and her family was written about in the story "Family Saga." Mary became the second wife of Hyrum Smith when his first wife, Jerusha, died. She was stepmother to five children and had two of her own. Having endured many hardships, she died in Utah on September 21, 1852 at age fifty-one.

Hyrum Smith was the older brother to the Prophet Joseph Smith. Several years after this story took place he was martyred with the prophet at Carthage Jail.

Top Photo: *Hyrum Smith*
Bottom Photo: *Mary Fielding Smith*

Chapter Twenty-Two
JONATHAN

Jonathan sat in the tabernacle chairs reserved for general authorities, wondering when it would be his turn to speak. His countenance was serious and sad, bespeaking a lifetime of toil. He was a nervous man who tended to be pessimistic and to worry.

Jonathan thought back to his lifetime of experiences, wondering which of them he might share in his talk today. After all, it wasn't his way to write down a talk beforehand. His mind worked in "motion-picture fashion" and that's how he preached, too. He shifted in his seat. His health had been poor lately, but he was still here.

Now more comfortable, Jonathan mused about his late revered father. Often he quoted from his father's wise sayings or told stories from his father's life. Jonathan's father, a pioneer, lived faithfully through trials to the end, and Jonathan hoped he could do as well. When Jonathan was fifteen his father died, forcing him to quit school to help provide for his mother, brother and sister. He became a mule driver—as good a one as could be found, he proudly remembered! Later he became a contractor, digging cellars or hauling rock or freighting. There were no regrets because he had always been completely honest and fair with his customers.

Through his teenage years his mother sewed and kept boarders, even though they were forced to move from their mansion to a two-room house. After several years of "hustling" for every penny they just weren't making it.

Jonathan continued to reminisce. When he was twenty-three they left Salt Lake City to live near Bear Lake, struggling to build a successful cattle and horse ranch despite the blizzards and cold weather. He chuckled inside when he remembered their "nine months winter and three months late fall" each year. Yes, it was hard and they lived in poverty in the early years. Finally, out of dogged determination, they made a success of the operation. Well, it hadn't been so bad after all. There were fun times. He never missed a party or dance if he could help it.

Jonathan recalled all the years of his inactivity in the church after the death of his father. He had fancied himself "free" in those days. However, he made sure that prayers were said morning and night when he superintended the rough crew that cut logs in the canyon for the Logan Temple. And everyone took his turn, too.

It wasn't until the summer he was twenty-eight that Jonathan's life changed and he started down the road that had led him to his present situation. He would never forget the day that Karl G. Maeser came to his small town and recruited students for Brigham Young Academy. For an hour and a half Elder Maeser spoke under the influence of the Spirit, and Jonathan's life was never the same. From then on he hungered for an education, spiritual as well as secular. After that talk he lost all interest in caring for horses and cattle.

Immediately Jonathan began to save money to attend BYA. He sold some of his ranch possessions and went door-to-door selling washing machines. By winter he finally had the means to go, and he was excited to do so. He remembered how his mother moved to Provo and boarded him and his brother and others, to pay for their education. He and his brother also earned money hauling coal from Coalville to outlying areas and bringing vegetables back to Coalville.

Yes, Jonathan had been fortunate to be able to stay at BYA for two years. This, he reflected, was where he gained his testimony. Karl G. Maeser had been his inspiration.

When he was nearly thirty his mission call to the Southern States had come. Like many elders there, he contracted malaria. Jonathan had been so ill that the new mission president looked him over and decided he should go home early. The mission funds were tight and it would only cost them $24.00 to send him home alive, but three hundred to send him home dead!! But Jonathan believed that God would support him after all his sacrifices to come on a mission. He stayed and went home alive after all. Ruefully he noted that he could still feel the effects of the malaria at times.

He reminisced about his marriage to his pretty Jennie following his mission. Over the years they had certainly shared plenty of ups and downs. And for all their toil they had been paid in rich dividends—their three boys and three girls. Jennie had sure had a challenge getting along with a stubborn fellow like himself!

And what about his call to be mission president? What a learning experience that had been. Never had the Spirit been with Jonathan as during that time. And finally, the call to the Council of Seventies, with his beloved former mission president, B.H. Roberts.

As he aged, Jonathan became more reclusive, more of a loner. He was high-strung, nervous and thin-skinned. Why did the other general authorities sometimes criticize him for the things he said in his talks? Maybe they didn't know how sensitive he really was. Any criticism always hurt. Jonathan had acquired some bad habits of speech when he was a mule-skinner. The only thing those beasts seemed to understand was strong language, and lots of it! What an effort it was to "unlearn" all those words. The two little words that remained weren't even considered swearing, where he came from! Somehow he could never speak from his heart without their slipping out. Even so, he supported his brethren fully and knew that their chastening would make him a better man.

Jonathan's awareness of his own flaws made him the more tolerant of the "common man." He hated hypocrisy as much as he loved truth. And he loved the truth far more than convention. Some people said that he saw things as they really were instead of as they ought to be or as he might have wanted them to be.

Well, he'd better stop his reminiscing now. They had just announced him as the next conference speaker. The tall, thin, man with the sad face stepped to the pulpit. Immediately, throughout the audience, those who had slept through the last speaker sat up, became attentive, relaxed and smiled. He began to speak in his high, shrill voice:

"My brethren and sisters, I have been hanging on the hook so long during this conference that I am nearly exhausted. I have had some wonderful thoughts, but I have waited so long they have nearly all oozed out of me."

Jonathan continued, liberally spicing his talk with humor. His father had always said that when you want to give a baby medicine, "Just tickle it under the chin and down goes the medicine." Jonathan hoped that, like the tickle on the baby's chin, his humor would help the "medicine" go down more easily. Using humor "always seemed better to [him] than using force or too much persuasion." Hopefully he could restrain his language this time, because he was sincere in his testimony of the gospel and his desire to share it. After all, Jonathan Golden Kimball was the son of strong pioneers, Heber C. Kimball and Christeen Golden Kimball.

J. Golden Kimball was made a member of the first Council of the Seventy at age thirty-eight, on April 5, 1892. He served in this capacity for forty-six years until his death, September 2, 1938, at age eighty-five. He was known throughout the church for his wit and frank manner of speaking.

Photo: *J. Golden Kimball*

Chapter Twenty-Three
THE TURNER

He was a craftsman. A wood turner, he used a foot-powered lathe to make rounded chair posts and legs, bed posts, table legs, drawer handles, etc. On the wall of the turner's shop he had several different types of chisels to shape wood in an infinite variety of ways. His nature was to work carefully and methodically in everything he did. With his woodturning skills he made a good living for his family.

Yet religion was the focus of his life. When sixteen years old he became a lay Methodist "exhorter," traveling to different areas to preach. Now twenty-eight years old and an intelligent, refined man, he had met with a group of people in his town twice weekly for two years in Bible study. As the turner studied with the group, they recognized the elements that made up Christ's true church, particularly priesthood authority from God and gifts of the Spirit. They systematically studied each religion available to them, including Methodism, and realized that not one of them was in harmony with the biblical pattern. He and other members of the group fervently fasted and prayed that the Lord would send them a messenger with the true gospel, if such was on the earth.

Still, his wood turning was his livelihood. He was working in the turning shop attached to his house when a Mormon missionary, Elder Parley P. Pratt, came to call. The turner had heard of the Mormons. His neighbors and friends had told him how the Mormons fooled gullible people in the modern day, just as false prophets and quack religionists had deceived people throughout history. So when his wife opened their door to this missionary and then interrupted his concentration on his work to meet the man, the turner was less than happy.

119

Elder Pratt brought a letter of introduction from one of the turner's friends. The craftsman considered it an imposition on the part of his friend to ask him to listen to such a man. Yet out of courtesy he stopped to share a brief tea with the missionary. In their discussion, he told the stranger, "I do not know what to think about you Mormons. I do not believe any kind of fanaticism. I profess to be acquainted with the Bible, and...I shall not listen to anything in opposition to that word."

Yes, the turner was actively seeking for a messenger from God, but certainly this "Mormon" could not be him!

Given no encouragement from the turner, Elder Pratt left and stayed overnight at a public house. As he had no luck the next day in the area, he planned to move on. Before he left town he went one more time to the turner's house to say goodbye.

This time the turner asked more questions about the missionary's doctrine and queried him about his destination, which delayed his departure a few minutes. As they said their goodbyes a widowed neighbor lady knocked on the door. As she and the turner's wife conversed, the turner's wife mentioned that a Mormon missionary was about to leave their home and the area, not having had any success. She felt badly, as she wondered if perhaps he really was a man of God. The neighbor said that she felt the Spirit had prompted her to come to their house. She then invited the missionary to stay at her house, with rooms to preach in. He gratefully accepted.

This widow invited her friends and neighbors to come and hear Elder Pratt speak. So despite his initial reluctance, the turner was there listening night after night, as gospel truths were unfolded to the group. The turner became curious, and talked with Elder Pratt one time for over three hours, with the missionary proving all he said from the Bible, as the turner requested. The turner began to believe. He wrote down eight sermons Elder Pratt preached, and compared their doctrine with the Bible, as had done with so many other religions. For the first time he found nothing contrary to his scripture.

The seed of testimony grew in the turner's heart. He carefully and intelligently studied the Book of Mormon, believed it, went on to the Doctrine and Covenants and believed. The day came when he and his wife were baptized and received the Holy Ghost. Their earnest prayers had been answered.

Neighbors thought the couple must be crazy. Why, everyone knew about that money-digging Joe Smith! He'd even tried to fool people by walking on planks laid under the water. He was as wicked a man as could be found! But the convert ignored the prejudice. His gospel roots ran deep. He had searched for these truths for a long time, spent hours in scripture study, and knew the value of what he had found.

Months later the convert visited Kirtland and met the Prophet Joseph. This was in the spring of 1837, at a time when many were apostatizing from the church and had become embittered against the prophet. The convert had a visit from his missionary friend, and sadly, even Elder Pratt had become disaffected. Elder Pratt came to the convert and expressed his feelings that the prophet had erred. The convert quietly listened and when his friend had vented his feelings, he replied:

"I'm surprised to hear you speak so...Before you left [us] you bore a strong testimony to Joseph Smith being a Prophet of God, and to the truth of the work he has inaugurated; and you said you knew these things by revelation, and the gift of the Holy Ghost. You gave to me a strict charge to the effect that though you or an angel from heaven was to declare anything else I was not to believe it. Now, Brother Parley, it is not man that I am following, but the Lord. The principles you taught me led me to Him, and I now have the same testimony that you then rejoiced in. If the work was true six months ago, it is true today; if Joseph Smith was then a prophet, he is now a prophet."

Elder Pratt later repented. The convert never lost his hard-won testimony. Within two years of this Kirtland conversation he was made an apostle, and John Taylor became president of the church in 1880.

John Taylor was the third President of the Church. He served from October 10, 1880, to his death on July 25, 1887, nearly seven years. He was with the prophet Joseph in the Carthage Jail and was wounded there. His Presidency was filled with bitter persecution over polygamy, which forced President Taylor to go into hiding. There he became ill and died.

Photo: *John Taylor*

Chapter Twenty-Four
WILL

W ill craved recognition. After all, hadn't he been a trusted, close friend of the prophet Joseph? For the last two-and-a-half years of the prophet's life Will was with the prophet almost daily. He wrote letters for Joseph, recorded revelations for him, and served as his agent in business and real estate matters. He was truly in "the inner circle."

But Will was not a leader by nature. He was a loyal, work-horse follower. His quiet, self-effacing manner led people to ignore him or to take his talents and skills for granted, particularly after the prophet Joseph's death. On one occasion the minutes for a meeting show Brigham Young, John Taylor, Heber C. Kimball and Newell K. Whitney in attendance. At this meeting Will read letters from Parley P. Pratt, who was serving a mission in the East, to the brethren. But Will's name never appeared in the minutes! This was not an isolated incident—in church service his tireless contributions were often taken for granted.

Even though Will wouldn't blow his own horn, at times he was exasperated at the way others ignored his hard work. Will was one of the scribes to church leaders and even kept some of their journals. With all his duties he often worked seven days a week. At the end of one frustrating day he wrote in his journal:

I am a perfect slave to them [church leaders] all the while...Other men who don't do half the work have a great deal more money and good property for their comfort than I have and they seem to be extolled to the skies.

Despite his occasional frustration, Will continued to serve.

In one instance he was recognized for his efforts. When he crossed the plains with the vanguard company in 1847, he kept a meticulous journal of the country they crossed. This was to assist later travelers. However, he didn't stop there. After he had spent several days tediously counting every wagon wheel revolution to estimate mileage, he recommended to the leaders that a mechanical device be made to do the counting. He persisted in letting Brigham Young know how important this was, until Orson Pratt, a mathematician, was assigned to design the device. After Elder Pratt designed it, a mechanic was assigned to make the gadget, and it was installed on a wagon wheel. Once more, Will's contribution was brushed aside when the mechanic claimed it was his own invention.

Even so, for a time the "roadometer" enabled Will to rise out of obscurity. Because this invention recorded mileage, Will was able to write and publish "The Latter Day Saints' Emigrants' Guide," detailing the route from Winter Quarters to Salt Lake Valley. It contained a table of the distances between creeks, over mountains, etc. It listed every landmark along the way, such as streams or hills, with brief descriptions of each. In the guide, Will suggested good places for camp sites, and for finding water and animal forage. He informed the reader of the best places to cross the streams. In his guide Will mentioned how many miles each landmark was from Winter Quarters and how many more miles were left to the Great Salt Lake. Many people considered this guide indispensable for their westward journey and were willing to pay exorbitant prices to get their hands on one, even a well-used one. Will must have felt justifiably proud of this accomplishment. For once his efforts were recognized!

But as well-known as this guide was in pioneer days, today it is largely unknown. Will's name was rescued from obscurity because of one seeming small event.

He was traveling west on the journey from Nauvoo to Winter Quarters in April of 1846. The night of the fourteenth Will took his turn on watch. It was a busy night for him, as

cattle and horses repeatedly broke into people's tents and wagons. But the next morning his day was redeemed when Will
received word that his youngest wife, Diantha, had given birth
to a son. Full of joy at this news, he sat down and wrote these
words:

> Come, Come, ye Saints, no toil nor labor fear;
> But with joy wend your way.
> Though hard to you this journey may appear,
> Grace shall be as your day.
> 'Tis better far for us to strive
> Our useless cares from us to drive;
> Do this, and joy your hearts will swell—
> All is well! All is well!
>
> Why should we mourn or think our lot is hard?
> 'Tis not so; all is right.
> Why should we think to earn a great reward
> If we now shun the fight?
> Gird up your loins; fresh courage take.
> Our God will never us forsake;
> And soon we'll have this tale to tell—
> All is well! All is well!
>
> We'll find the place which God for us prepared,
> Far away, in the West,
> Where none shall come to hurt or make afraid;
> There the Saints will be blessed.
> We'll make the air with music ring,
> Shout praises to our God and King;
> Above the rest these words we'll tell—
> All is well! All is well!
>
> And should we die before our journey's through,
> Happy day! All is well!
> We then are free from toil and sorrow too;
> With the just we shall dwell!
> But if our lives are spared again
> To see the Saints their rest obtain,

> Oh, how we'll make this chorus swell—
> All is well! All is well!

These words were put to an old English tune, and thousands who followed Will across the plains took this as their theme song. We still sing it 150 years later and remember his name today. Generations of Saints have found courage, hope and faith through a song William Clayton wrote impulsively one cold April morning: "Come, Come, Ye Saints."

William Clayton was a British convert to the Church and served in the British Mission Presidency. He later emigrated to the United States, where the events in this story took place.

Photo: *William Clayton*

Chapter Twenty-Five

JENNETTA

Jennetta was a "golden contact." She visited a friend in Preston, England, one day. Fortuitously, Elder Heber C. Kimball came to visit this man's home while Jennetta was there. He was introduced to her as a Mormon missionary. Since she was the daughter of a minister, they began a spirited gospel discussion. He found her to be a very pleasant and intelligent young lady, eager to hear the doctrines of the restoration. Elder Kimball told Jennetta where and when he would be preaching that evening and invited her to come and hear him. She came to hear him preach that evening and the following evening as well. After these two meetings Jennetta was fully converted to the gospel and asked to be baptized.

Elder Kimball baptized her in the River Ribble and confirmed her on its banks. Jennetta went to her home in neighboring Walkerfold and introduced the gospel to her family. Soon her father, who was the minister there, requested the elders to preach in his church. This opened many doors to the missionaries and they baptized many in the area. Then they began baptizing too many in his own fold, and his opinion of them changed. He quickly turned very anti-Mormon. Jennetta, however, remained steadfast.

Elder Kimball had several fellow laborers in the vineyard, among whom was one named Willard. Willard happened to have the same last name as the new young convert. The same day Heber C. Kimball baptized Jennetta, he wrote to Willard (laboring in another area) and said prophetically: "Willard, I baptized your wife today!" One can only guess at Willard's surprise when he read this.

Jennetta's baptism was in August and Willard didn't

proselyte in her area until the next March. When he and Elder Kimball again met, Elder Kimball urged Willard to meet this girl who shared his last name. It was probably by design and not accident, that Willard soon arranged to be at a convert's home where he would run into Jennetta. Apparently this was their first meeting, and Willard wrote of it:

> While walking in Thornly I plucked a snowdrop, far through the hedge, and carried it to James Mercer's and hung it up in his kitchen; soon after Jennetta ... came into the room, and I walked with her and Alice Parker to Ribchester, and attended meeting with Brothers Kimball and Hyde at Brother Clark's.
>
> While walking with these sisters ... I remarked, '[our common last name] was a good name—I never want to change it, do you, Jennetta? 'No, I do not,' was her reply, and I think she never will.

In between Willard's missionary duties, the two courted for several months. Jennetta's minister father strongly opposed their relationship because of his anti-Mormon feelings. In September of that year, when Jennetta was twenty-one and of legal age to make her own decision, she and Willard were married. By then the apostles had left the mission for America, leaving Willard as first counselor to the mission president.

Even before they were married, Willard had been called to the apostleship. Yet no one else in England knew about this for some time, except he himself, to whom it was revealed. He wasn't ordained until Brigham Young and the rest of the twelve came to England nearly two years after his being called. Willard didn't have to go through the trials and persecution that the apostles in America faced. Still, he had his own peculiar brand of trials in England, and felt that they were a result of his calling.

One of his trials was his relationship with the people in the Preston branch of the church. Willard's new wife, Jennetta, was pretty, cultured, well-educated and came from a wealthy home. This contrasted sharply with the mostly poverty-stricken membership of the branch. The English people were very class-conscious, and she was from the upper class. The other converts were generally from the lower classes. Jennetta's family had told her from the beginning that she was too good to associate with these common people. But Jennetta was not as bothered by the differences as were the branch members. She was aware of their jealousy and tried to fit in. She was used to wearing a veil and carrying a muff in cold weather. She found that these and her other fine clothes offended branch members. So she left them at home and made it a point to wear the worst clothes she had, but these were still too good in the people's eyes. When she and Willard each were sick a lot for a time, the branch members superstitiously attributed that to Satan's influence.

Jennetta was very ill at one time and the "Saints" criticized her husband for staying by her side instead of going out to preach. They criticized Jennetta for missing church on the days when she didn't feel well enough to go that far. Many in the branch gossiped that Willard shouldn't have married in the first place while on his mission. (Indeed, the talk had started during their courting). It reached the point that virtually all of the elders in Preston were against the couple. There was in the branch a serious spirit of "jealousy, tattling, evil-speaking, surmising, covetousness, and rebellion."

Finally, tired of the backbiting and faultfinding, Willard stood at the pulpit. He asked anyone in the branch who had complaints against him or Jennetta to come to him and talk things over so that he could apologize if necessary. Only one man came. He acknowledged that he was in the wrong because he'd judged without any proof.

Jennetta was a gentle soul and was patient through all of this. She lived in a no-man's land, rejected by her own family as well as her "church" family, but she still remained true to the gospel and to her beloved. Willard felt that his call to the apostleship was behind everything, and we can surmise that after that was publicly made known, he and Jennetta rose somewhat in the estimation of the branch members.

The day came when the two left England for America and Nauvoo. When she was only twenty-seven years old Jennetta became very ill. Willard gave up all his other work to stay by her side for several weeks, until she died.

Jennetta was the wife of Willard Richards, the seventeenth apostle called in this dispensation.

Jennetta Richards married Willard Richards, who was later ordained an apostle. They had three children, one who died in infancy. Willard served several missions and was second counselor to Brigham Young. He was with the Prophet Joseph in Carthage Jail at the time of the martyrdom and escaped unhurt.

Photo: *Heber John, Willard and Jennetta Richards*

Chapter Twenty-Six
WANTED

W ANTED: DEAD OR ALIVE. These posters hung on
the walls of post offices in the "Wild West." But
before the "Wild West" was, lived a man who spent most of
his days being "Wanted." He never had his face on a poster,
yet few have ever been hounded and pursued by as many people over so long a period of time. Those who hunted him
thought they would be doing the world a favor by killing him,
whether by legal or extralegal means. As a result he was
almost constantly on the run, but he was strong and athletic
and could usually get away if he had enough warning. What a
difficulty it would be if he had to slow down for one not as
hardy as he.

One night he had his nine-year-old cousin with him as he
sat down to eat at a friend's house. They'd barely finished their
meal when a mob gathered outside threatening them and
demanding that their host bring his guests out to them. But the
host had his wits about him and helped them out through the
back door and led them away in the night.

The mob soon realized they'd been tricked and had men
ride along the road they thought the two cousins would take.
They lit bonfires and hunted through the area for the escapees.
But the man with his young cousin took another route through
the woods. The bonfires that were lit to help their enemies,
instead helped them by lighting their way.

The young boy's energy was soon exhausted by fear and
sickness, and now the hunted man had to decide whether to
leave his cousin to be captured by the mob or to help him
along, endangering himself. It would not be the boy the mobbers would want: They wanted only the man. Still, who knew

what those kind of men would do? The man decided to risk his life, and carried the boy through the night on his shoulders, resting periodically. It was hours before they came back to the road and soon afterwards they were home. The boy was grateful to the man who had saved his life by risking his own.

This was only one of many close escapes the man had, different only because of the extra burden of helping his young cousin. The man often wondered if he would live to complete his work. Then his dying father gave him a blessing in which he told him that he would live to fulfill his mission on earth. The son, overcome, wept, and asked him, "Oh, Father, shall I?" He could hardly believe from day to day sometimes that he still survived despite all the persecution. How grateful he was for the assurance in that blessing.

From the time he was in his youth until his death at age thirty-eight he was "wanted" dead by many, and as he went to the last jail in which he would be incarcerated, he knew that this time those who sought his life would succeed. He said repeatedly that he was going "like a lamb to the slaughter."

After his murder his mother cried out in anguish, "Why?" The answer given her was that he was taken to God that he might at last have rest. Though his life had been short, his trials had been many and certainly if anyone deserved rest it was he.

His murderers thought that by killing him they had ended his "evil" work, but they were wrong. His adherents, who carry forth what he started, today number over nine million and are growing every day.

Of course, the man who was hunted and hounded was the Prophet Joseph Smith.

Joseph Smith was the founder and first prophet of the Church of Jesus Christ of Latter-day Saints. He translated the Book of Mormon. He served as prophet from April 6, 1830, until his martyrdom on June 27, 1844, fourteen years. He "has done more, save Jesus only, for the salvation of men in this world, than any other man that ever lived in it." (D&C 135:3).

Photo: *Joseph Smith*

Chapter Twenty-Seven
LOVE THE THIRD TIME
AROUND

Who would have paired these two? He was sixty-one years old, father of eleven, twice a widower, with a public persona that was serious and doctrinaire, a strait-laced scriptorian. She was thirty-five years old and never before married, free-spirited, energetic, and joyful. Their marriage was his third and her first.

She was cheerful, vivacious and outgoing. She loved being in the limelight, front and center stage, while he felt more comfortable standing in the wings, quiet and retiring. He was comfortable with nearly constant work, while she knew how to have fun, taking him to musical events and movies.

She loved him for his courtliness and kindness. He was proud of her beautiful singing voice and her willingness to share her talents with others. When he spoke at meetings, she came along and sang, warming up his audience with her music. In time, she convinced him to sing often with her, sitting by her side on the piano bench as she accompanied. She called these "duets;" he jokingly called them "do its." Being with her was always fun.

He had always taken life pretty seriously, especially during the past few years. His second wife, mother of nine of his children, had become ill. The last few years before her death were hard on her as well as her family. Medical help was sought. Spiritual help was implored. Yet the illness was intense and painful for all involved. He had become even more serious and worked harder these past few years. Yet now again he was blessed, as he had been with each previous wife, with one who could love him and help lift his burdens.

His new wife went tooling down the highway in her little car, telling him she had special permission from the highway patrol to speed. He felt a carefree sense of renewal when with her.

His office was close to their apartment. One day, she got out her "spy glass" and viewed his office, where resided a bust of his grandmother. She called him to teasingly ask, "Who is that woman in your office?" She carried on conversations with a friend as she stood on her second-floor balcony, the friend standing on the sidewalk below, and then tossed her friend an orange for good luck. She was adept at dispensing good cheer.

Once he told his son: "[This wife] always belonged to me. I know that the Lord intended it. And the Lord sent her to me when I needed a wife and needed help and somebody in the family to help us and take care of us, and the Lord had raised her up and sent her to me. And oh, how grateful I am, for she has been just as true and faithful as anybody could possibly be, and we all love her."

Once soon after the couple married, the church president and his wife came to visit. The next day the prophet wrote to the husband: "I was delighted last night to hear you and your good wife sing. I am thankful to think that you are going to take a little bit of time to sing and visit with your loved ones, instead of working, working, working. I am sure that the singing will prolong your life...I want you to prolong your life."

Indeed, the balance brought to his life by this helpmeet did seem to prolong his life. He was made church president when he was ninety-three years of age and passed away when he was nearly ninety-six. Although his third marriage was his longest (thirty-three years), he outlived even this wife by nearly a year. He was Joseph Fielding Smith and she, Jesse Ella Evans Smith.

Joseph Fielding Smith was tenth President of the Church. He served for two-and-a-half years in that capacity, from January 23, 1970 to July 2, 1972. During his life he wrote twenty-five books, including several Church doctrinal works. Keenly interested in Church history, he served as Church Historian for sixty-four years.

Jesse Ella Evans Smith was a noted contralto who sang with the Mormon Tabernacle Choir, often as a soloist.

Photos: *Joseph Fielding Smith and Jesse Ella Evans Smith*

Chapter Twenty-Eight
KARINE

K arine and John loved each other very much, but it was
an even greater love that brought them together, for
each loved the truth.

They met when John became the twenty-one-year-old
schoolmaster on Karine's Norwegian island. She was his
twelve-year-old pupil. Though John knew right away that he
would marry her someday, it was many years before he proposed. He waited until she was nineteen. She accepted, but
they waited nearly another three years for him to further his
education before they married.

After their marriage John taught school in their home. But
teaching children wasn't enough. He wanted to educate the
fishermen on their island, whose idle hours were spent mostly
in drinking and card-playing. In order to do this he built a
community center where he could expose the people of the
island to great books, to ideas, to music. Religion was important as well: On Sundays he read the Lutheran service there.
His life's work was helping people to learn and gain greater
enjoyment.

In time a baby boy, Andreas, was born to John and Karine.
John's ambition for greater educational and cultural opportunities moved them to the Norwegian mainland. Life seemed full
of possibilities.

When Andreas was nearly six years old another son,
Osborne, came to them. Their future seemed assured. But
within weeks of Osborne's birth the young father suddenly
became very sick and died within days. Karine's world was
turned upside down. She was a widow at age twenty-eight,
with two small sons to raise. She and John had hoped their

145

sons would continue their father's work by becoming teachers and serving others as he had done. Now, educating these sons would be her responsibility alone. All her hopes for the future now rested in her boys.

John's death stimulated much pondering, prayer and Bible study for Karine. She had so many questions: Was God just? Why had her husband been taken from her? What was the meaning and purpose of life?

One day one of her sons needed his shoes repaired. The shoemaker's son picked up the shoes and returned them a few days later with Mormon tracts in them. These aroused Karine's curiosity. The next time she needed shoes repaired she walked to the shop herself, hoping to ask the shoemaker about the church. Not knowing the shoemaker personally, she was too shy. As she opened the door to leave the shop, he spoke to her hesitantly.

"You may be surprised to hear me say that I can give you something of more value than soles for your child's shoes."

Karine answered doubtfully, "What can you, a shoemaker, give me better than soles for my son's shoes? You speak in riddles."

"If you will but listen, I can teach you the Lord's true plan of salvation for His children...I can teach you whence you came, why you are upon earth, and where you will go after death."

Karine was confused. "Who are you?"

"I am a member of the Church of Christ—we are called Mormons. We have the truth of God."

She recoiled at the word. Mormons! Quickly she thanked him and left. Yet she couldn't dismiss the shoemaker's testimony. The next time shoes came back they again held Mormon pamphlets.

Karine's curiosity mounted and one Sunday she courageously attended a Mormon meeting. It was held in a room on the second floor of the shoemaker's home. Most Norwegians were very class-conscious, Karine included, and she could not imagine joining such a humble group. Yet in the coming months, as a battle raged inside Karine, she finally decided that truth was the only important issue here. If it were true she would join, regardless of class. After all, wasn't it the love of truth that had bound her and John together and made learning so important to them both?

Karine argued doctrines, point by point, with the missionaries and with the shoemaker. She prayed and struggled with these new gospel concepts for two years. Karine knew this was the truth, and she was baptized in the icy fjord.

Now Karine was rejected by her own family as well as John's. Their old friends also ostracized her. The church members became her family and friends.

Karine considered moving to Zion, weighing its effect on her sons' futures. She was committed to the goal that they would enjoy the educational opportunities she and John had planned together. They must follow in his footsteps. Two years after her baptism, she weighed the risks and made the move.

In Utah their circumstances were greatly reduced. Even though they lived in poverty for a while, educating her sons was always on Karine's mind. Andreas finished grade school in two years, working odd jobs at the same time. Then he went to work full-time, and was tutored in the evenings. After three years of this, his job was working out so well that it looked as if he could soon support the family on what he made. Yet Karine still had her dream of higher education for him, bolstered by evidence that he seemed to be unusually gifted intellectually.

Karine's bishop objected to her desires for more education for Andreas. After all, she was just a poor immigrant woman and should be content with her present circumstances. Karine told the well-meaning bishop that the Lord had sent her sons to her, not him, to raise. She predicted that one day he would admit she'd been right, and one day children would universally have a chance for higher education.

Karine mortgaged her home and borrowed money from

friends who believed in her son's potential. She sent Andreas to Brigham Young College and then to Harvard, where he did very well.

The time came when Andreas supported her as well as his missionary brother, Osborne. Andreas hungered for learning. He wanted still more education, so he borrowed money to study in Europe. With his exceptionally brilliant mind Andreas followed in his father's footsteps, using his talents to bless others. Upon returning to Utah he worked on college faculties and then became a college and university president. He'd hardly known his father but John was still Andreas' ideal of what a good teacher should be, and of how he could influence others in a positive way. Following his father's example, Andreas initiated outreach programs to educate adults throughout his community. Karine had taught him that education was only of value when used to serve one's fellow man.

Osborne, too, became educated and served as a college professor; however, he died while still a young man.

Karine was so proud of her sons. They'd carried on the great educational work John had loved so much. Because of her conversion her sons grew to love not only secular truths but spiritual ones as well. Karine's testimony remained firm and she was always thankful for the humble shoemaker's message. Her full name was Anna Karine Gaarden Widtsoe, and after her death, her son, John Andreas Widtsoe, became an apostle.

Karine's son, John A. Widtsoe, became President of the Utah State Agricultural College, and then the University of Utah until his calling in 1921 to be an apostle. He served in that calling for thirty-one years. Elder Widtsoe wrote several agricultural and church books and edited the book "Brigham Young's Discourses."

Top Photo: *John A. Widtsoe, Anna Karine Widtsoe, and Osborne Widtsoe*
Bottom Photo: *John A. Widtsoe*

Chapter Twenty-Nine
HEALED

The apostle had always been close to his younger brother. Since they enjoyed frequent visits, the apostle was glad to house his brother for the night when the spring thaw prevented the brother from reaching his own home. It was 1916; the thaw had turned the canyon river into a torrent, washing out the road through the canyon. So the younger brother, anxious to reach his home farther up the canyon, called his wife and asked her to have someone bring a horse down the next morning.

Morning came, and the apostle offered, instead, to take his brother up the canyon as far as possible, until they reached the point where the road was washed out. As they got in the car the apostle had a strong impression that he should go only to the bridge, then turn back.

They were late starting and the apostle must get to work, so he drove as fast as his Model T would go.

As he approached the bridge he remembered taking his children up the road just the day before. They'd been able to safely cross the bridge and go a little farther before the road was washed out. The bridge this morning seemed to be fine, just as it was the day before. He discounted his impression, pressed the gas pedal, and sped over the bridge.

Suddenly his younger brother yelled out, "Oh, look out! There's a rope!"

The night watchman had stretched a rope taut across the road and the day watchman hadn't yet come to take it down.

The apostle's reflexes weren't fast enough. He reached for the emergency brake, but not in time. The rope broke the windshield and threw back the canvas top, hitting him right in the chin, tearing his face, knocking out teeth, and breaking his lower jaw. His passenger ducked and wasn't hurt. The driver lay semiconscious.

His younger brother quickly moved the apostle over, got in the driver's seat, and headed back down the canyon road to the hospital, where his injured brother went into surgery.

After the surgery one of the hospital staff said, "Too bad; he will be disfigured for life."

Another suggested the apostle might grow a beard to hide his scars. A close friend came to visit and walked right by his room without recognizing him. After finding him, the visitor said as he left, "Well, the eyes are the same, anyhow." Otherwise the patient was unrecognizable.

Three brethren who were close to the apostle soon were at the hospital to administer to him. In the blessing he was told that he wouldn't be disfigured or have any pain.

A few days later Heber J. Grant, President of the Twelve, stopped to see the apostle. President Grant told him not to try to talk, that he was just there to give him a blessing. In the blessing he promised that all scars would disappear. After the blessing, in looking closely at his friend, President Grant thought: "My, I've made a promise that cannot be fulfilled!"

Seven months later, the patient and President Grant were seated close to each other at a banquet, and President Grant once more looked closely at his friend's face. From his vantage point he said he couldn't see a scar anywhere on the apostle's face.

The second promise came to pass as well—there was no pain during the recuperation. The patient even wondered if the rope had injured his facial nerves, until he accidentally bumped the facial stitches with his arm, causing great pain.

His recovery was miraculous and complete. With his tall, stately bearing, full head of white hair, and handsome smiling face, people often remarked that David O. McKay truly looked like a prophet.

David O. McKay was the ninth President of the Church. He was sustained on April 9, 1951 and died January 18, 1970, serving nearly nineteen years. He was known for his sayings, "No other success can compensate for failure in the home," and "Every member a missionary." In 1963 he celebrated his ninetieth birthday. At that time more than half of the church's membership had not known another prophet.

Photo: *David O. McKay*

Chapter Thirty

THE DANCE

Bishop Edwin D. Woolley was pretty strict about the dances held in the Thirteenth Ward. In the other Salt Lake City wards only three "round dances" (waltzes) were allowed per evening, perhaps on the theory that they allowed the partners too much close contact. The rest of the dances were square dances. But Bishop Woolley felt that even three round dances were too many and allowed none at all in his ward parties.

There was a band called Olsen's Quadrille Band which was the only band able to play the 'Blue Danube Waltz' well, and the teenagers loved to dance to that. But once in the Thirteenth Ward the flute player in the band was drunk, and from that time on, Bishop Woolley hadn't allowed Olsen's band to play in the ward.

In those days (the mid-1870's) the buildings had only bare wood boards for floors. In other wards, the youth whittled wax candles before the dances and waxed the floor. However, in this ward, strait-laced Bishop Woolley wouldn't allow that, either, saying he didn't want people falling down and breaking their necks!

Not surprisingly, after all these restrictions were placed on the Thirteenth Ward dances, none of the "younger generation" wanted to come any more. Certainly they could find more fun elsewhere, and Thirteenth Ward dances began to lose money.

The winter before the St. George Temple was finished, every Salt Lake City ward had a party to raise funds for completing the temple. All the wards were planning dances, and Bishop Woolley's competitive spirit came to the fore. His pride was on the line. After all, the Thirteenth Ward led the other wards in everything they did, and he wanted to be able to donate the most money to the temple. Perhaps he realized that he must loosen up some in order to do this. Reluctantly, the bishop called in a popular young man from his ward to plan this important party.

Fortunately, this particular young man had superb confidence and negotiating skills and was not intimidated by the bishop. Perhaps the teenager was also aware that under the current circumstances, the bishop would be willing to compromise his principles just a little. The conversation went like this:

Bishop Woolley: "I want you to organize a party. You have more friends among the young people than anyone. I want you to choose your own committee and arrange the whole thing. Make a success of it. We generally lead every other ward in everything we try to do. I want you to be sure to beat them all."

Young man: "I'll do my best, but you'll have to agree to pay the loss if there is one."

BW: (Swallowing hard) "Loss?"

YM: "Yes, you can't have the party in our ward and make any money. The young people won't come any more. In other places they allow them to have three round dances, and you won't have any. I'd rather dance three round dances and throw all the rest away. You've got to have three waltzes."

BW: "All right. Take the three waltzes."

YM: "You won't allow Olsen's Quadrille Band. They're the only people who can play the 'Blue Danube Waltz' well. That draws a crowd. They have the finest cornetist in Salt Lake who will give some cornet solos during the evening."

BW: (Sighing) "Take Olsen's Quadrille Band; take your three round dances; wax your floor!"

YM: "There's something else. You won't allow a Gentile to come. I would like the United States Marshall and one or two high-principled gentlemen to come and let them see how Mormon boys and girls can behave themselves. There will be no rowdyism. This will be a crowd of the finest kind of young people."

BW: (Defeated) "Invite whom you please."

YM: "I'm going to charge $1.50 instead of $1.00."

BW: "Oh, the people won't pay that!"

YM: "Yes they will, with Olsen's full Quadrille Band."

So the planning for the dance went forward. The young man diplomatically chose the bishop's son as his assistant and they chose a committee. Then they went to work, buying the finest tickets possible. Large pictures of Brigham Young and other general authorities were mounted on the wall. They waxed the floors in the dancing area and put down carpets in the sitting area. Using their contacts at ZCMI and the railroad they convinced employees to buy tickets. Brigham Young's family members were invited to come. The enterprising young committee head sold tickets to local businessmen.

The night of the dance President Young showed up, asking, "This is for the benefit of the St. George Temple, isn't it?"

The young man answered, "Yes."

Brigham Young plunked down ten dollars. "Is that enough to pay for my ticket?"

The young man answered, "Plenty." He didn't know if President Young expected any change, but none was offered!

As the night went on, the three permitted round dances were finished, but the youth on the committee had prepared a surprise. They planned a fourth round dance, a waltz quadrille. In this dance the couples waltzed within a square, such as square dancers use. Before the quadrille began, the audacious young planner went to sit by President Young to see what he would say. The dance began. Puzzled, President Young turned to this young man. "They're waltzing."

He replied, "No, they're not waltzing; when they waltz they waltz all around the room; this is a quadrille."

Brigham Young laughed and said: "Oh, you boys, you boys."

Well, the dance was popular, and successful financially, too. Even Bishop Woolley must have been happy with the outcome, because the next day he personally took over $80.00 in proceeds to Brigham Young. No other ward even came close. His able young helper was Heber J. Grant.

At the time of this story Brigham Young was the second President of the Church. Heber J. Grant would later become the seventh President.

Photo this page: Brigham Young
Photo next page: Heber J. Grant

BIBLIOGRAPHY

CHAPTER ONE: THE GOOD HUSBAND

Arrington, Leonard J. *Brigham Young, American Moses.* Urbana and Chicago: University of Illinois Press: 1986

Arrington, Leonard J. and Madsen, Susan Arrington. *Mothers of the Prophets.* Salt Lake City: Deseret Book: 1987

England, Eugene. *Brother Brigham.* Salt Lake City: Bookcraft: 1980

CHAPTER TWO: THE REFUGEE

Miner, Caroline Eyring, and Kimball, Edward L. *Camilla: A Biography of Camilla Eyring Kimball.* Salt Lake City: Deseret Book: 1980

CHAPTER THREE: THE PROPHET AND HIS FRIEND

Barrett, Ivan J. *Joseph Smith and the Restoration: A History of the LDS Church to 1846.* Provo: Brigham Young University Press: 1973

Doctrine and Covenants Student Manual. Salt Lake City: Corporation of the President of The Church of Jesus Christ of Latter-day Saints: 1981

Holland, Jeffrey R. "I Stand All Amazed." *Ensign* (August 1985): Vol. 15 No. 8 (pp.71-72)

Ludlow, Daniel H. *A Companion to Your Study of the Doctrine and Covenants Volume II.* Salt Lake City: Deseret Book: 1978 (pp. 368-69)

Smith, Joseph. *History of the Church of Jesus Christ of Latter-day Saints.* Edited by B. H. Roberts. 2nd edition. Salt Lake City: Deseret Book: 1980. Vol. 4

CHAPTER FOUR: THE HERD BOY

Kenney, Scott in *The Presidents of the Church*, Edited by Leonard J. Arrington. Salt Lake City: Deseret Book: 1986

Nibley, Preston. *Pioneer Stories.* Salt Lake City: Bookcraft: 1976 (pp. 17-21)

Rich, Russell R. *Ensign to the Nations.* Provo: Brigham Young University Publications: 1972 (p. 94)

CHAPTER FIVE: JEDDY

Gibbons, Francis M. *Heber J. Grant: Man of Steel, Prophet of God.* Salt Lake City: Deseret Book: 1979

Gordon, Arthur. *A Touch of Wonder.* New York: Berkley Publishing Group: 1974

Hinckley, Bryant S. *Heber J. Grant: Highlights in the Life of a Great Leader.* Salt Lake City: Deseret Book: 1951

Hinckley, Gordon B. "Believe His Prophets." *Ensign* (May 1992) Vol. 22 No. 5, (p. 51)

Walker, Ronald W. in *Presidents of the Church*, Edited by Leonard J. Arrington. Salt Lake City: Deseret Book: 1986

West, Emerson R. *Profiles of the Presidents.* Salt Lake City: Deseret Book: 1972

CHAPTER SIX: THE GREAT ESCAPE

Pratt, Parley P. *Autobiography of Parley P. Pratt.* Salt Lake City: Deseret Book: 1985

CHAPTER SEVEN: NORA

Esplin, Ronald K. "Sickness and Faith, Nauvoo Letters." *BYU Studies.* 15:4:425-34.

Gibbons, Francis M. *John Taylor: Mormon Philosopher, Prophet of God.* Salt Lake City: Deseret Book: 1985

Roberts, B.H. *The Life of John Taylor.* Salt Lake City: Bookcraft: 1963

CHAPTER EIGHT: THE PRINCIPAL

Arrington, Leonard J., Editor. *The Presidents of the Church.* Salt Lake City: Deseret Book: 1986

Gibbons, Francis M. *Harold B. Lee: Man of Vision, Prophet of God.* Salt Lake City: Deseret Book: 1993

CHAPTER NINE: JOSEPH

Smith, Lucy Mack. *History of Joseph Smith by His Mother.* Salt Lake City: Bookcraft: 1958. (pp. 48-50)

CHAPTER TEN: HARRY

Madsen, Truman G. *Defender of the Faith: The B.H. Roberts Story.* Salt Lake City: Bookcraft: 1980

CHAPTER ELEVEN: THE PROPHET

Kimball, Stanley B. *Heber C. Kimball.* Urbana and Chicago: University of Illinois Press: 1981

Whitney, Orson F. *The Life of Heber C. Kimball.* Salt Lake City: Bookcraft: 1945

CHAPTER TWELVE: THE STUDENT

McCloud, Susan Evans. *Not in Vain: The Inspiring Story of Ellis Shipp, Pioneer Woman Doctor.* Salt Lake City: Bookcraft: 1984

CHAPTER THIRTEEN: THE FISHERMAN

Gibbons, Francis M. *Wilford Woodruff: Wondrous Worker, Prophet of God.* Salt Lake City: Deseret Book: 1988

CHAPTER FOURTEEN: FAMILY SAGA

Bloxham, Moss and Porter, Editors. *Truth Will Prevail.* Cambridge, England: LDS Church: 1987

Corbett, Don C. *Mary Fielding Smith; Daughter of Britain.* Salt Lake City: Deseret Book: 1974

Evans, Richard L. *A Century of "Mormonism" in Great Britain.* Salt Lake City: Publishers Press: 1937

Roberts, B.H. *The Life of John Taylor.* Salt Lake City: Bookcraft: 1963

CHAPTER FIFTEEN: GOTTFRIED

Burton, Alma. *Karl G. Maeser: Mormon Educator.* Salt Lake City: Deseret Book: 1953

CHAPTER SIXTEEN: THE VISITOR

Dew, Sheri. *Ezra Taft Benson: A Biography.* Salt Lake City: Deseret Book: 1987

CHAPTER SEVENTEEN: INDOMITABLE LADY

Arrington, Leonard J. and Madsen, Susan Arrington. *Mothers of the Prophets.* Salt Lake City: Deseret Book: 1987

Smith, Lucy Mack. *History of Joseph Smith by his Mother.* Salt Lake City: Bookcraft: 1958

CHAPTER EIGHTEEN: THE PASTOR AND HIS FRIEND

Peale, Norman Vincent. "A blessing from President Kimball." *Ensign* (February 1977): Vol. 7 No. 2, (p. 84)

CHAPTER NINETEEN: LUCY'S FRIEND

Gibbons, Francis M. *George Albert Smith: Kind and Caring Christian, Prophet of God.* Salt Lake City: Deseret Book: 1990

Pusey, Merlo J. in *The Presidents of the Church.* Edited by Leonard J. Arrington. Salt Lake City: Deseret Book: 1986

CHAPTER TWENTY: SHARING CULTURE

Beecher, Maureen Ursenbach. "The Polysophical Society: A Phoenix Infrequent." *Encyclia.* 1981: Volume 58: Page 145.

Gibbons, Francis M. *Lorenzo Snow: Spiritual Giant, Prophet of God.* Salt Lake City: Deseret Book: 1982

Romney, Thomas C. *The Life of Lorenzo Snow.* Salt Lake City: Sugarhouse Press: 1955

Snow, Eliza R. *Biography and Family Record of Lorenzo Snow.* Salt Lake City: Deseret News Company: 1884

Swinton, Heidi S. in *The Presidents of the Church,* Edited by Leonard J. Arrington. Salt Lake City: Deseret Book: 1986

CHAPTER TWENTY-ONE: A JAIL VISIT

Corbett, Don C. *Mary Fielding Smith: Daughter of Britain.* Salt Lake City: Deseret Book: 1974

CHAPTER TWENTY-TWO: JONATHAN

Cheney, Thomas E. *The Golden Legacy: A Folk History of J. Golden Kimball.* Santa Barbara and Salt Lake City: Peregrine Smith, Inc.: 1974

Richards, Claude. *J. Golden Kimball: The Story, Sayings and Sermons of a Unique Personality.* Salt Lake City: Deseret Book: 1951

CHAPTER TWENTY-THREE: THE TURNER

Bealer, Alex W. *Old Ways of Working Wood.* Barre: Barre Publishing Company: 1980

Gibbons, Francis. *John Taylor: Mormon Philosopher, Prophet of God.* Salt Lake City: Deseret Book: 1985

Pratt, Parley P. *Autobiography of Parley P. Pratt.* Salt Lake City: Deseret Book: 1985

Roberts, B.H. *Life of John Taylor.* Salt Lake City: Bookcraft: 1963

Taylor, John. *The Gospel Kingdom.* Salt Lake City: Bookcraft: 1943

CHAPTER TWENTY-FOUR: WILL

Allen, James B. *Trials of Discipleship: The Story of William Clayton, a Mormon.* Urbana and Chicago: University of Illinois Press: 1987

Cornwall, J. Spencer. *Stories of our Mormon Hymns.* Salt Lake City: Deseret Book: 1980

Hymns of the Church of Jesus Christ of Latter-day Saints. Salt Lake City: Church of Jesus Christ of Latter-day Saints: 1985

CHAPTER TWENTY-FIVE: JENNETTA

Bloxham, Moss, and Porter, Editors. *Truth Will Prevail.* Cambridge, England: LDS Church: 1987

Evans, Richard L. *A Century of Mormonism in Great Britain.* Salt Lake City: Deseret News Press: 1937

Ludlow, Daniel H. *A Companion to Your Study of the Doctrine and Covenants.* Vol. 2 Salt Lake City: Deseret Book: 1978

Noall, Claire. *Intimate Disciple: A Portrait of Willard Richards.* Salt Lake City: University of Utah Press: 1957

Whitney, Orson F. *The Life of Heber C. Kimball.* Salt Lake City: Bookcraft: 1945

Writings of Early Latter-day Saints and Their Contemporaries, A Database Collection. Milton V. Backman and Keith W. Perkins, Editors. Provo, Utah: Religious Studies Center, Brigham Young University, 1992 (*Autobiography of Willard Richards*)

CHAPTER TWENTY-SIX: WANTED

Corbett, Pearson H. *Hyrum Smith: Patriarch.* Salt Lake City: Deseret Book: 1971

Smith, John Lyman. "He Carried Me." *The New Era* (December 1992): Vol. 22 No. 12, p. 38

Smith, Lucy Mack. *History of Joseph Smith by His Mother.* Salt Lake City: Bookcraft: 1958

CHAPTER TWENTY-SEVEN: LOVE THE THIRD TIME AROUND

Gibbons, Francis M. *Joseph Fielding Smith: Gospel Scholar, Prophet of God.* Salt Lake City: Deseret Book: 1992

CHAPTER TWENTY-EIGHT: KARINE

Widtsoe, John A. *In a Sunlit Land.* Salt Lake City: Deseret News Press: 1953 Published by Milton R. Hunter and G. Homer Durham

Widtsoe, John A. *In the Gospel Net.* Salt Lake City: Improvement Era Publication: 1941

CHAPTER TWENTY-NINE: HEALED
Allen, James B. in *Presidents of the Church*, edited by Leonard J. Arrington. Salt Lake City: Deseret Book: 1986
Middlemiss, Clare, compiler. *Cherished Experiences from the Writings of President David O. McKay.* Salt Lake City: Deseret Book: 1955
World Book Encyclopedia. Chicago: Field Enterprises: 1977 Volume "A" (pp. 924-25, "Automobiles")

CHAPTER THIRTY: THE DANCE
Gibbons, Francis M. *Heber J. Grant: Man of Steel, Prophet of God.* Salt Lake City: Deseret Book: 1979
Grant, Heber J. Gospel Standards. Salt Lake City: Improvement Era Publication: 1943 (pp. 280-82)

(Used in general biographical information):

West, Emerson R. *Profiles of the Presidents.* Salt Lake City: Deseret Book: 1972
Deseret News, *1995/1996 Church Almanac.* Salt Lake City: Deseret News: 1994